WELCOME TO BILLINGS
PARDNER

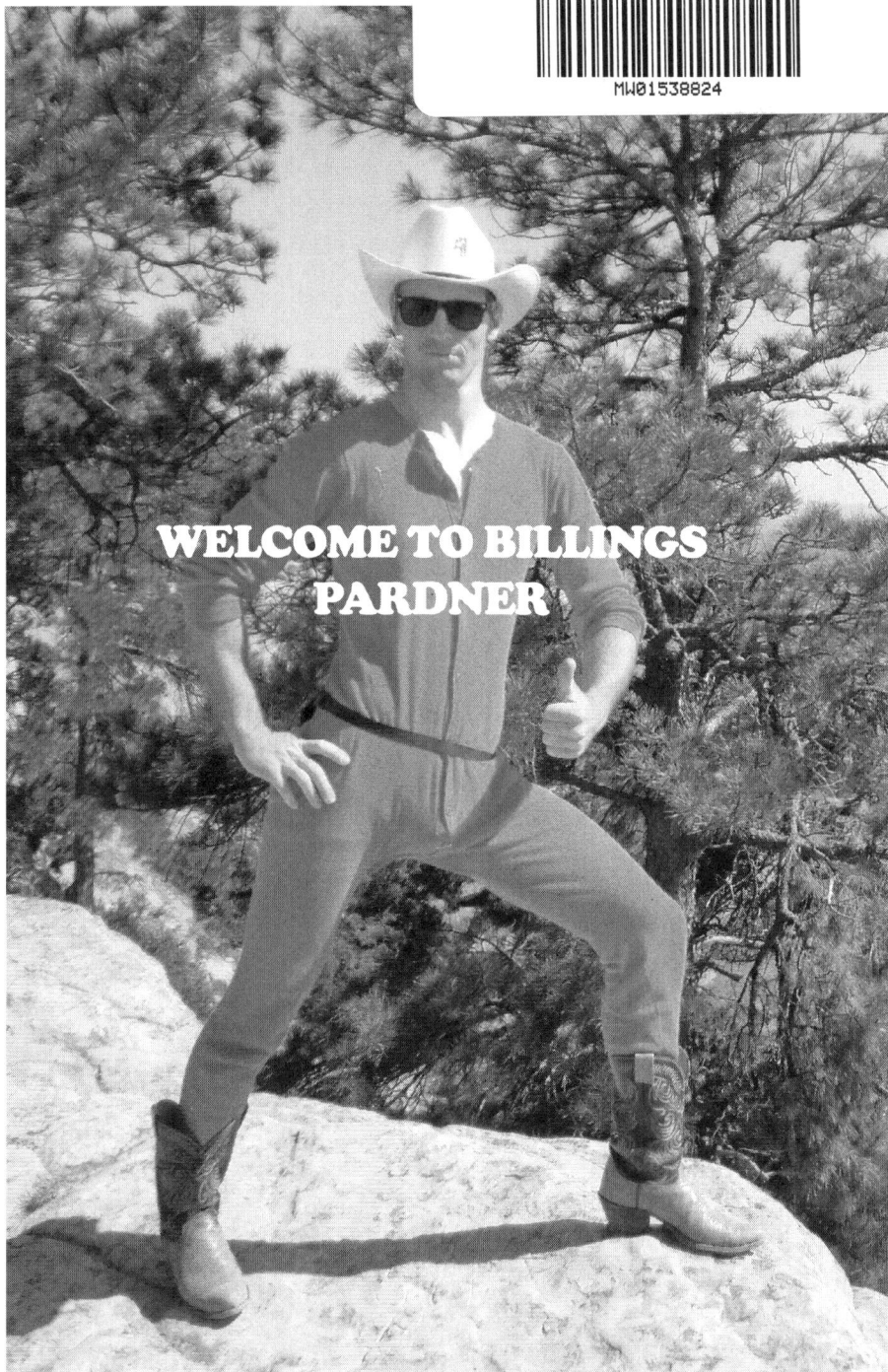

SUPER SAND LAND

Climbing Entertainment System

A guide to rock climbing in Billings Montana
by Joel Anderson

Castles made of sand, fall into the sea, eventually

-Jimi Hendrix

Disclaimer

Climbing is Dangerous
The activities described in this book are potentially dangerous. Rock climbing involves unavoidable risks including the risk of serious bodily injury and death. All forms of wilderness recreation have a higher level of risk than many ordinary activities. These risks include but are not limited to slips, falls, falling objects, equipment failure, being injured by equipment both properly and improperly used, automobile accidents, insect and animal attacks, accident or illness in remote places, forces of nature, effects of weather, rockfall, and other hazards of traveling in mountainous terrain, as well as accidents resulting from fatigue, exercise of poor judgment, and inexperience.

Conditions Change
This book contains compilations of verified and unverified climbing route information gathered from many different and often completely unreliable sources. Although some of this information is intended to assist climbers in locating and following climbing routes, it is neither represented nor guaranteed to be accurate or complete. Rimrock conditions change from day to day and season to season, rendering any information subject to change without warning. Do not trust your personal safety to any information presented here. Climbing safely depends on your own good judgment, based on experience and a realistic assessment of your climbing ability, weather, and route conditions. However, given all of the potential hazards of rock climbing, safety cannot be guaranteed even in the exercise of perfect judgment.

Seek Proper Instruction
Those lacking climbing experience should seek professional training and hire a guide or enroll in a climbing instruction course before venturing into the mountains on their own. The author and publisher of this book do not assume any responsibility or liability for your safety.

Those who use this information, do so at their own risk.

MAIN MENU

Thanks

The ever flowing and sometimes ethereal Billings climbing community should thank themselves for their determination and desire in making the best out of the sandy beast that is the Rims. The following people have made significant contributions to the Billings climbing community through anchor placement, route development, and / or helping with the creation of this book.

Chad Chadwick
Brian Hagerty
Mike Abbey
Rusty Willis
Jim Rott
Chris Talbot
Ari Greenberg
Loren Rausch
Aaron Ten Harmsel
Lis Ten Harmsel
Charles Barron
Thad McGrail
Joe Schmechel
Ben Hoiness

Plus the many others before me I unfortunately never had the opportunity of meeting.

Check out http://billingsclimbingguide.blogspot.com for corrections, updates, and sharing any new routes for the next edition, because there is a lot of rock in Billings and the best routes are still to be found.

+ Joel Anderson, October 2012

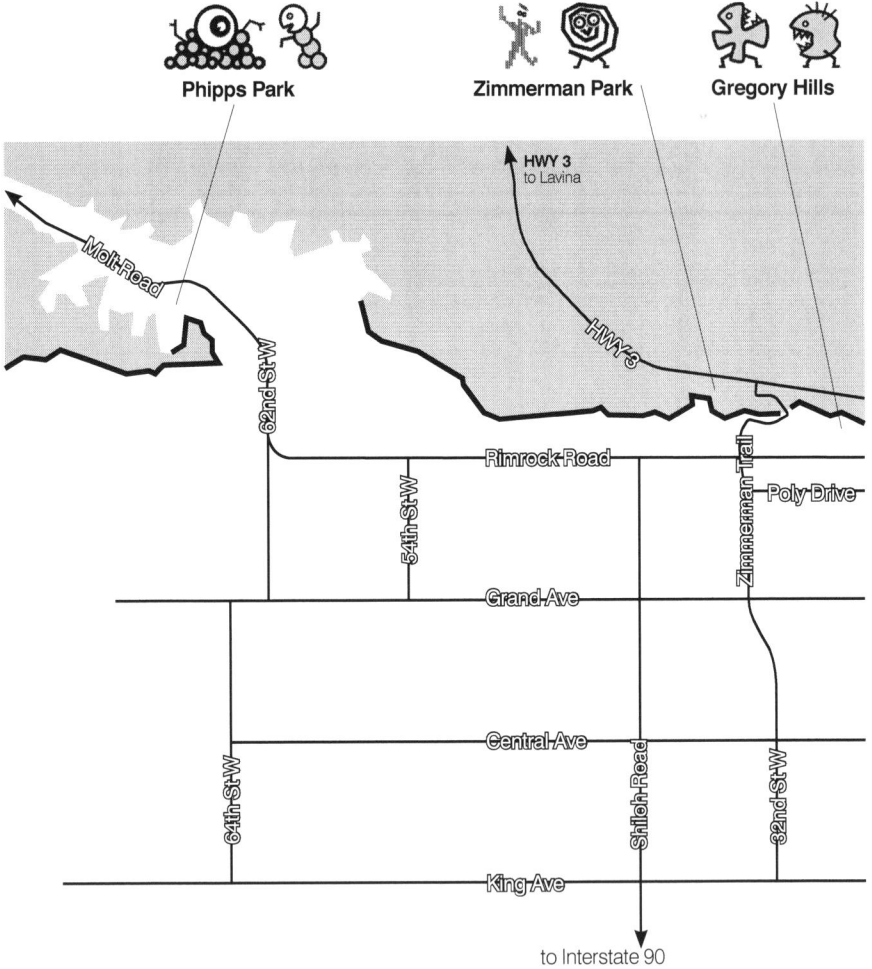

Phipps Park

Zimmerman Park

Gregory Hills

HWY 3
to Lavina

Molt Road

62nd St W

HWY 3

Rimrock Road

54th St W

Zimmerman Trail

Poly Drive

Grand Ave

Central Ave

64th St W

Shiloh Road

32nd St W

King Ave

to Interstate 90

Arvin Boulders   Water Tower

Country Club

Steepworld Climbing Gym

HWY 87
to Roundup

Yellowstone River

AIRPORT

HWY 3

Main St

Rimrock

Poly Drive

17th St W

15th St W

to Miles City
Sheridan, WY

6th Ave N

4th Ave N

13th St E

Grand Ave

24th St W

5th St W

1st Ave N

**Downtown
Billings**

The Basecamp

Montana Ave

N 27th St

Sacrifice Cliffs
climbing not permitted

Central Ave

Laurel Rd

King Ave

INTERSTATE 90

South Hills

to Bozeman

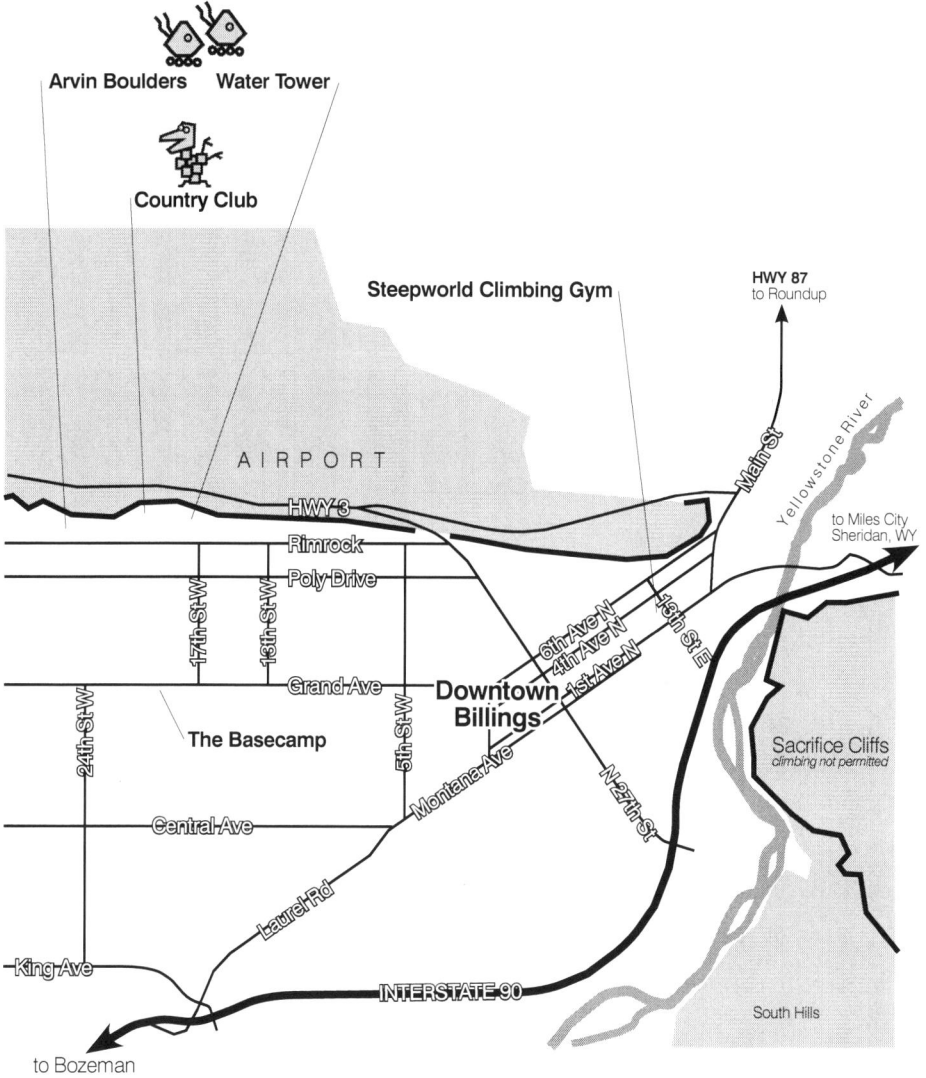

N
O THE SAND LAND KINGDOM
Billings, Montana, USA

9

SAVE THE SAND LAND KINGDOM

The Sand Land Kingdom is being held captive by the Crazy Henchmen of the Evil Sand Monster. It's up to you to use your super climbing powers to rescue the kingdom from the Sand Monster before time runs out! Defeat the evil henchmen controlling each world of to save Sand Land and earn yourself the right to square off against the Sand Monster himself.

Crackasaurus
Gregory Hills Crack Climbs

CrimperStein
Gregory Hills Face Climbs

SloperZilla
Phipps Park Boulders

SloperZilla Jr.
Phipps Park Junior Boulders

The Dirt Dorks
Arvin and Water Tower Boulders

Abominable Crack Man
Zimmerman Park Crack Problems

Beastly Dust Devil
Zimmerman Park Face Problems

RimRock Dragon
Country Club Boulders

Evil Sand Monster
Boss Level

ABOUT THE RIMS

Why
Because it's there. From everywhere in Billings you can see the rims. Few towns can boast of the urban rock climbing experience like we have in Billings. You can be trad climbing or bouldering 5 minutes after work. While the rock can be questionable at times, it does provide a unique climbing experience within the Montana Wyoming region. The crack climbing is easy on the hands and the bouldering rewards those with a diversity of skills. The purpose of this book is to provide good beta to help the climbing community grow into something we all can be excited to be a part of.

Access
Much of the actual cliff-bands that make up the rims is owned by the city and considered parkland. Climbers should always access the rims from open access points and not cross private property. This can be difficult due to many legal access points being unmarked and unfortunately for boulderers, private property lines below the rims typically extend to the base of the cliff line. There are occasional parkland designations where there are occasional breaks in private property for uphill access. Access to the rims from above is best done via Zimmerman Park or the public parking off of Highway 3 across from Billings Logan International Airport.

Rimrock Sandstone
Rimrock Sandstone is a soft sandstone and varies from worthless to better than you were expecting. Orange rock tends to be the most solid, while white and black rock tends to be sandy and dirty. Notes have been made regarding potential poor rock you might encounter, but holds will break and routes will change. Pull down, not out. Do not use wire brushes, be careful with nylon brushes. Aggressive cleaning can cause permanent damage. Let the rock dry out after a rain, as it is severely weakened by moisture. Prevent rope scars by correctly placing top rope anchors over the edge.

Seasons
Climbing is possible all year long on the rims, with the best seasons being fall and spring. Summers can get quite hot, thus most climb early in the day or later in the evening. Due to their southern exposure it can feel 10 degrees warmer on a sunny winter day making climbing possible even on 40 degree days.

Trundling
Many areas described in this book lay above homes. While the risk is very minimal of an accident happening, it goes without saying, do not throw or trundle blocks from the top or the base of any climbs.

Ethics
Even though the rock quality may be dubious, this does not give us permission to use dubious ethics. Breaking off loose rock is acceptable when cleaning a newly found boulder problem, but chipping, creating holds, or manufacturing routes in rock is NEVER OK. Our attitude should always be to elevate ourselves to the boulder problem, not degrade the boulder problem to our ability. If you can't climb it, leave it for later, when you're stronger, or smarter, or for the next generation.

5.11b — Nay, it's a crack climb, 5.9

The Star System

Star Ratings go from 0 to 4. The star system evaluates the objective quality of a boulder problem. These qualities are; clear start & finish, clear or proud line, quality of rock, no glue or chipping, quality of landing, and history of the problem or route.

Flora and Fauna

Poison Ivy is common along the rims. Birds and Bees nest in cracks. Rattlesnakes are common and will be found in the sun on cold days, and in the shadows on hot days. If you get bitten, go to the emergency room. Deer commonly roam the rims and mountain lions have even been sighted along the western rims (Zimmerman and Phipps).

Steepteam is a 501c3 non-profit organization dedicated to providing climbing mentorship and training to Billings area youth interested in improving their climbing skills through practice and competition.
www.steepteam.com

Climbing Gyms and Gear Retail

Steepworld
Bouldering gym, lessons, and retail store. 12-9 Mon-Fri 10-6 Sat Closed Sun
208 North 13th Street
406-25-CLIMB

Basecamp
Retail store. 9:30-8 Mon-Fri 9:30-6 Sat 11-5 Sun
1730 Grand Avenue
(406) 248-4555

Eats and Drinks in Billings:

Unless you're into chain restaurants, downtown, the 2nd & Broadway area or Montana Avenue is a good place to start.

Water Tower

Where

From downtown, take Rimrock Road west. Turn left onto Stanford Drive and head up the hill. Park at the intersection of Stanford Drive and Oak Knoll Place, do not block the closed road. Hike up the closed road that takes you to the water tower and the boulders.

The clean steep cracks in the rims directly above the water tower go in the 5.11 range.

Access

The water tower and boulders reside on city land.

The Dirt Dorks

Climb these problems at the Arvin and Water Tower boulders to defeat the Dirt Dorks.

[ ] Kettle Cooked Thin Chips V0   [ ] Arvin Traverse V3
[ ] Lucks and Locks V1   [ ] Potential Energy V4
[ ] Slap Happy V1   [ ] Mega Arete V4
[ ] Full Curl V2   [ ] Man the Rails V4
[ ] Macerated V3

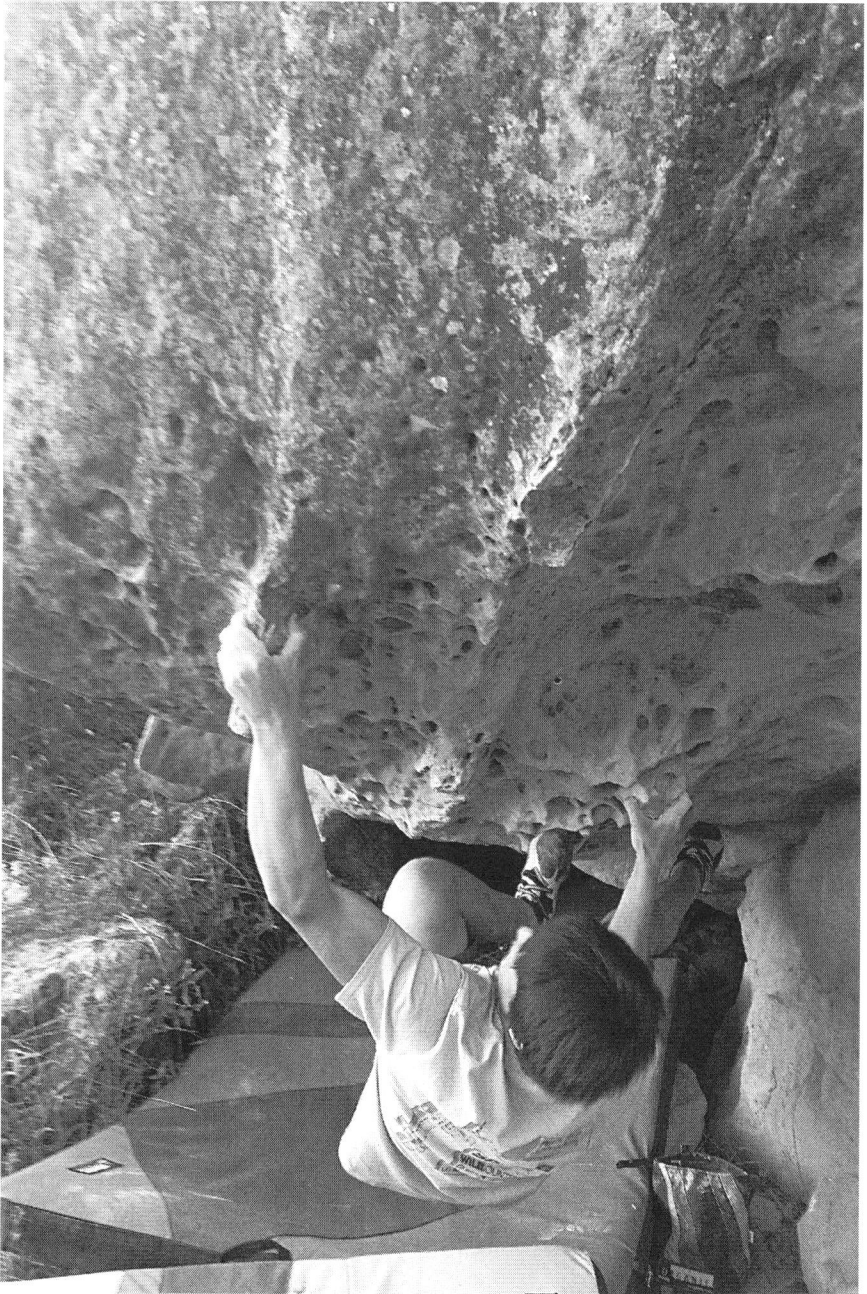

Charlie Barron climbs Rocky Top Orange Soda

Water Tower Boulder
Located at the top of the service road just west of the Water Tower.

1. Potential Energy V4***
Start on the sloping ledge, move up to a great crimp and throw right to the arete and pull yourself around the corner.

2. To the Point V5**
Start the same as for Potential Energy but when at the great crimp move straight up to the right lip towards the top of the boulder instead of out right.

3. Power Tower V7***
Start as for Potential Energy and take the line straight to the top via a sidepull crimp or dyno.

4. Sloping Lip V8*
Climb the left arete of the boulder.

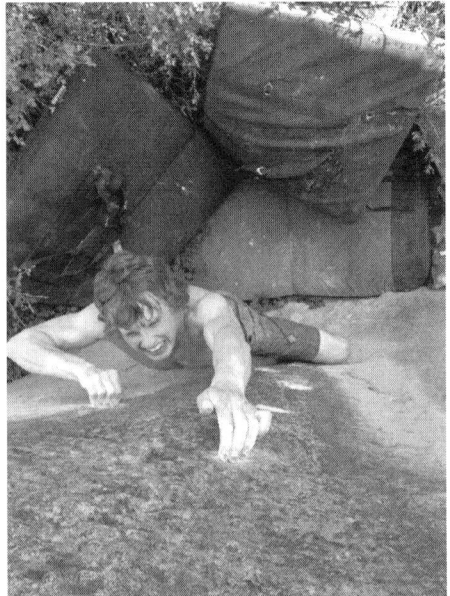

Kerrek Stinson climbing Rave Ambition on the Mega Arete Boulder (photo Charlie Barron)

The Wave Boulder
located above the water tower

1. Full Curl V2**
Start on the sloping ledge and traverse up left on the lip of the wave.

2. Wipeout V7*
Start on small crimpers at the base of the wave and climb out. The rock at the base provides an awkward fall zone and dab potential.

Arrowhead Boulder
located west of the Water Tower Boulder

1. Thuggin' V2**
Stand start. Climb the sharp cut triangular face of the boulder using little chips and the aretes.

2. Thuggin' Sit Start V8**
Sit down start on side pulls and bad feet.

The Party Pit
This boulder faces west, resting in an alcove just west of the Water Tower Boulder.

1. Party Pants V1***
Start in the underhanging seam and connect the fingerlocks to the top.

2. Proof to Party V7
Start low left and traverse the sloping rail to top out at the high point. For those that can't get enough sloping traverses.

Eastside Boulders

These boulder lay east of the water tower up a small hill.

Sandhill Boulder

This will be the first boulder you encounter after heading east from the water tower.

1. Jug Traverse V1

Start on the sloping ledge and move up right avoiding dabbing the boulder below.

2. Happy Fun V0**

These are the finishing moves to "The Gift of Knowledge." Start on the obvious two hand ledge.

3. The Gift of Knowledge V6*

Start on the arete, move out to slopers, then pull up to jugs and top out. Awkward landing zone.

4. Kettle Cooked Thin Chips V0*

Start on the same arete as The Gift of Knowledge but instead move straight up and right using thin crimps and a nice jug out left.

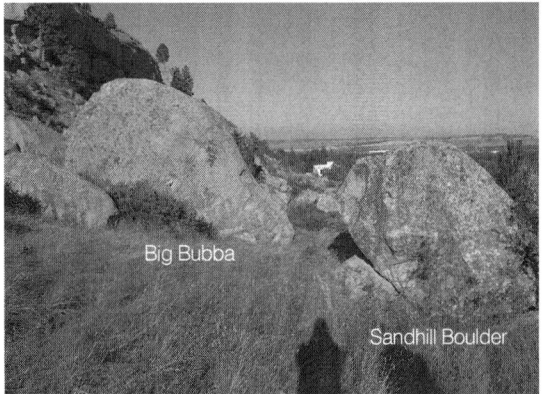

Big Bubba

A big boulder. The south face has been climbed. The west face looks interesting......

Rocky Top Boulder

This boulder lies above and slightly east of Big Bubba.

1. Rocky Top Orange Soda V5****

This thing is for real. Steep overhanging juggy pockets and fins on solid rock, well, as solid as rimrock can get. Sit start down low in fingery pockets and climb up to a big throw and a slopey lip.

Big Bubba

Sandhill Boulder

Mega Arete Boulder

This beautiful boulder is a 5 minute hike on the footpath west from the Water Tower Boulder. The boulder sits next to the trail, you can't miss it.

1. Mega Arete V4****
A Billings classic. Stand start low on the obvious rail and climb up using the rail and crimps out right. Wonderful technique based problem on one of the most unique climbing features in Billings.

2. Rave Ambition V7***
Climb the thin crimps on good rock.

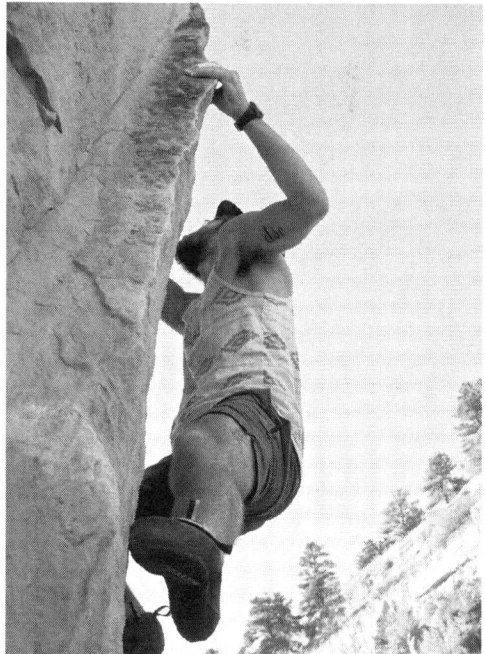

Dillon Key handling the sweet rail on Mega Arete

19

Arvin Boulders

Where

The Arvin Boulders are actually located below the Rims at a turn in Granite Avenue. Take Arvin north off of Rimrock Road till it turns left into Granite Avenue. Drive west on Granite Avenue till it turns south back down the hill. Park at the turn. The boulders lie up the hill just off the road.

Access

The Arvin Boulders sit on a vacant lot via a narrow access point and are very close to two homes. All climbers should maintain a minimal impact in the area. This means pick up any trash, quiet voices, no boom boxes or stereos, positive language, climb in small groups, respect the neighbors privacy, and proper parking of automobiles in the street. Do not climb or explore the boulders west of the Arvin Boulder as they are on private property.

Man the Rails Boulder
This is the first boulder closest to the road.

1. Man the Rails V4**** Sit start in the hand crack. Move up and right, traversing along the edge of the boulder and top out up the southern prow. Super Classic, one of Billings best.

2. Over the Top V1** Sit start in the crack as in Man the Rails but go straight up to top out.

3. Left Hook V6 Sit start on the horn on the lip and traverse right into Man the Rails on dirty slopers.

4. Heath Bar Crunch V8*** Start on chalked rails down low and go up thin holds to finish on the top half of Man the Rails.

5. Project Traverse left from supporting boulder into the finish of Man the Rails.

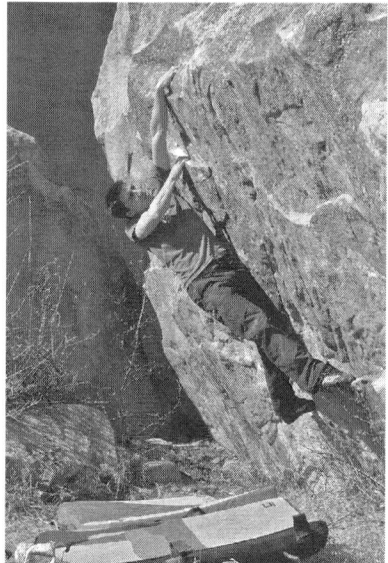

Aaron Ten Harmsel on the Arvin Traverse.

Arvin Boulder
East Face

The next boulder west of the Man the Rails Boulder. While not on their property, this boulder is nearly in the neighbors backyard. Out of respect, avoid climbing on this boulder if the family is visible, and always keep your voices low.

1. Slap Happy V1** Start on a sloping ledge on the arete and climb left up the arete without exiting right onto the slab down climb.

2. Macerated V3*** Start on crimps and move up on more full and half pad crimps. The top moves can be dusty.

3. Macerated Sit Start V6* Sit start to Macerated starting on two wide undercling sidepulls.

4. True Grit V4* Climb the arete, holds in the left crack are off.

5. Paper Back V1** Climb the crack.

Chris Hayes on the Arvin Traverse (photo: Rausch collection)

Arvin Boulder
southwest face

1. Transformation V5** Sit down start on a pinch hold on the right side of the arete. Climb up the arete and exit left on good holds.

2. T's Arete V6 Same start as Transformation but this time top out directly above the arete skipping the good holds out left.

3. Right Mantle V1* Stand start and mantle up.

4. Center Mantel V4* Start on the long rail in the center of the face. Huck straight up and top out.

5. Arvin Traverse V3**** Start on two decent holds near the left side of the face. Go up and traverse right across the lip and top out using the finishing hold of T's Arete. One of Billing's best.

6. Undertow V3* Sit start as for the Arvin Traverse but climb straight up.

7. Lower Traverse V8*** Start on Transformation and traverse the boulder avoiding all holds on the lip to Undertow and top out.

8. Pinch Project V7* Start the same as for the Arvin Traverse but move up, right, and top out.

Country Club

Where

Approach from above the rims: From downtown, take Highway 3 northwest out of town past the airport towards Lavina. 1.5 miles past the airport roundabout on the left there will be a 4-5 car pullout with boulders defining the edge. Park here. Hike west and down into the ravine along a trail (Meyers Trail) that will take you below the rims. After you get below the base of the Rims there will be a telephone pole on the crest of the ridge, hike to the pole. From there head down and left, looking for a subtle game trail that will take you through the dense thicket and over to the boulders on the other side of the ravine.

Approach from below the Rims: From downtown, take Rimrock Road west. Turn left on Country Club Circle and drive up the hill. Park at the vacant lot near the top of the hill, as of spring 2012 a house is planned to be built here. Take the trail or the utilities alley between the private lots up towards the rims. Before you get to the base of the Rims there will be a telephone pole on the crest of the ridge, hike to the pole. From there head down and left, looking for a subtle game trail that will take you through the dense thicket and over to the boulders on the other side of the ravine.

The obvious crack lines on the Rims along the trail have been climbed and range from 5.9-5.11

Access

The Country Club area sits on city owned parkland, but is close to residences. A low profile is always recommended out of respect to neighbors.

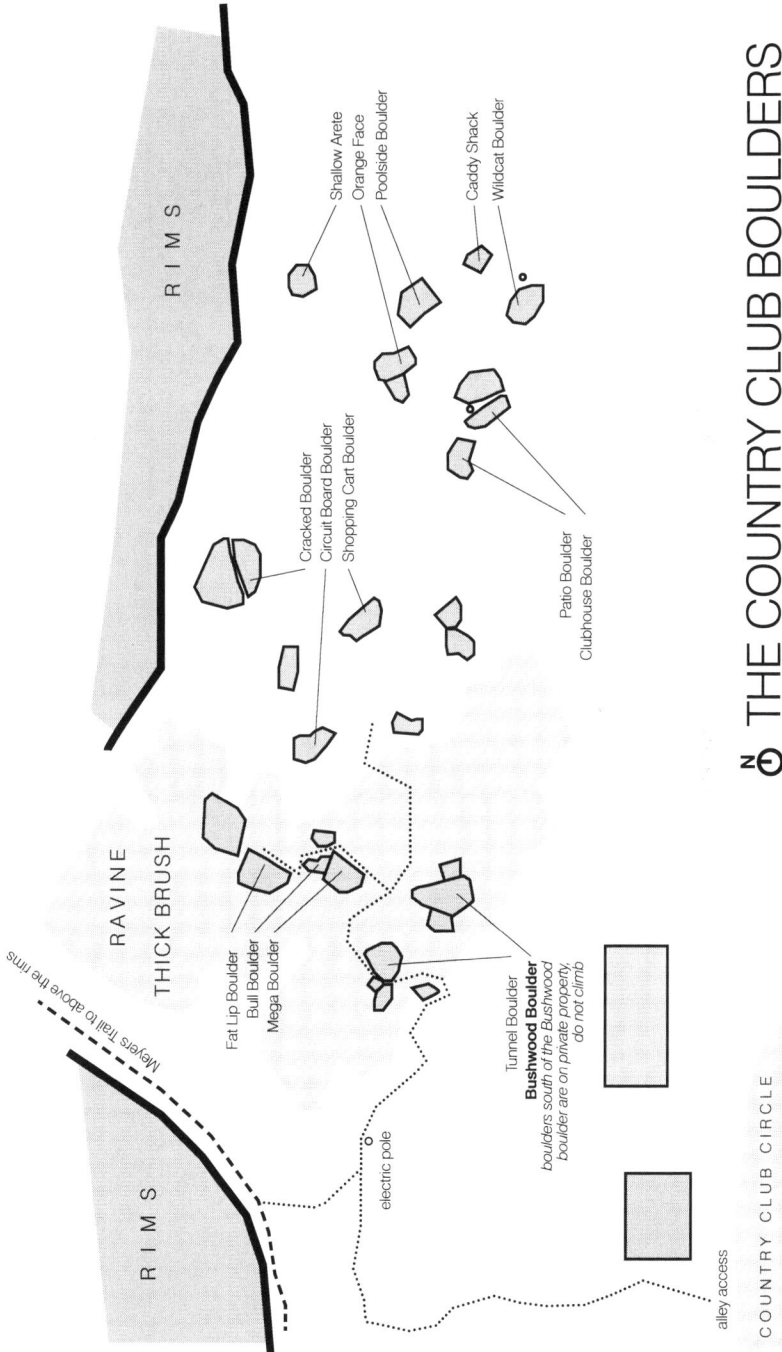

THE COUNTRY CLUB BOULDERS

N

RIMS

RIMS

RAVINE

THICK BRUSH

COUNTRY CLUB CIRCLE

Meyers Trail to above the rims

electric pole

alley access

Shallow Arete
Orange Face
Poolside Boulder

Caddy Shack
Wildcat Boulder

Cracked Boulder
Circuit Board Boulder
Shopping Cart Boulder

Patio Boulder
Clubhouse Boulder

Fat Lip Boulder
Bull Boulder
Mega Boulder

Tunnel Boulder
Bushwood Boulder
*boulders south of the Bushwood
boulder are on private property;
do not climb*

Clubhouse Boulder

1. Slopers in My Face V2*
Start on a nice slopey ledge. Work up right to the McLovin Feature and finish out left on crimps.

2. McLovin! V4***
Start the same as Slopers in My Face and work up and through the slopey McLovin feature to a big toss up right and top out.

3. Obsidian Thoughts V8/9 **
Start on left hand undercling and right hand crimp at head height. Figure out the move to finish on McLovin!

4. Sand in My Eye V7**
Start on a small sloping edge and climb up to the fantastic super crimp feature and move out right to finish on Slam Dunk.

5. The Super Crimper V8***
Start the same as the Sand in My Eye but when you get to the super crimper hold throw up to the lip and top out.

6. Slam Dunk V3**
Start on a nice jug and climb / huck for the top lip and top out. Holds around right of the arete are off.

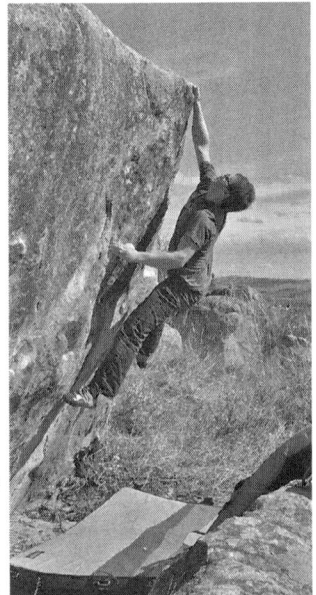

Joel Anderson sticking Slam Dunk

Wildcat Boulder

1. Wildcat V1**
Start on the nice ledge and make the big move to the next level.

2. White Russian V1*
Start low on the arete and climb up and left into the starting ledge of Wildcat.

3. Pokey & Smokey V3
Start as for Wildcat and move out to the left arete and top out the slab.

4. Britches & Ditches V0*
Climb the face right of White Russian. Needs more cleaning.

Rimrock Dragon
Defeat Rimrock Dragon by climbing these problems at Country Club.

[ ] Club Crack V0
[ ] Wildcat V1
[ ] Chopping Block V1
[ ] Slopers in My Face V2
[ ] Two Hams Traverse V2

[ ] Lips V2
[ ] Left Circuit V3
[ ] Slam Dunk V3
[ ] McLovin! V4

Patio Boulder
This boulder lies immediately west of the Clubhouse Boulder.

1. Chopping Block V1*
Start in the crack down left and traverse right through the face and stem up around the block. Good rock below but the easy topout needs more cleaning.

The Bull Boulder

This boulder oozes efflorescence that can be cleaned quickly to give you a solid texture to climb on.

1. Taurus Nose Ring PROJECT
Start on the nice ledge, make the big move up left to the big hole, and top out through the crack. Needs some cleaning.

2. Dimples PROJECT V-HARD
Start as for Wildcat and move out to the left arete and top out the slab.

3. Soap Scum V1
Climb the face, tall finish.

Little Calf Boulder

This boulder lies across from the Golf Ball Boulder and hosts a nice lowball traverse.

1. Ten Hams Traverse V6
Start low left and traverse right across the lip and top out around the corner.

2. Two Hams Traverse V2*
The shorter version of Ten Hams. Exit early at the good jug.

Aaron Ten Harmsel climbing Long Lips

Circuit Board Boulder

The first boulder you find when you come into the clearing. Excellent sharp cut sandstone.

1. Left Circuit V3***
Start on a decent rail with bad feet and move up and left to top out.

2. Lips V2**
Start on the sharp lip, traverse left near the end and mantle up.

3. Long Lips V4***
Start as for Lips and traverse to the arete and use the arete and left face to top out.

4. Daddy Long Lips V5**
Start as for Lips, traverse into the start of Left Circuit, and top out.

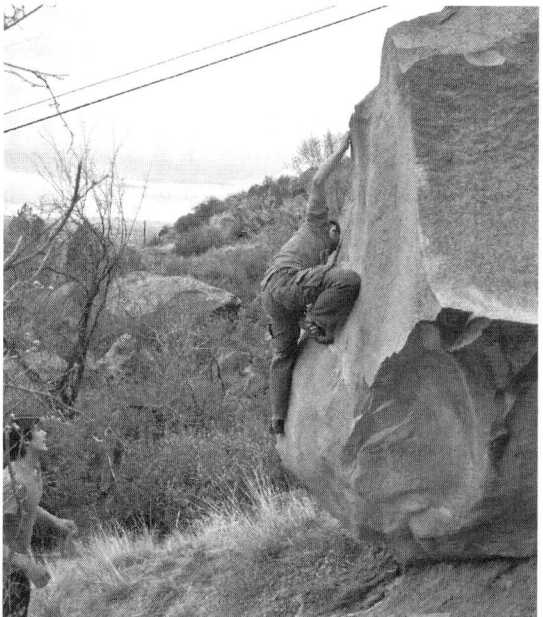

Aaron Ten Harmsel climbing Left Circuit.

Poolside Boulder

A smaller sized boulder north of the Clubhouse Boulder.

1. Warm Up V0*
Start low right and traverse up the lip.

2. Club Crack V0**
Sit start, climb the crack.

Shallow Arete

This boulder lies up the hill from the Poolside Boulder. Great rock, big boulder, messy landing, bring lots of pads.

1. The Shallow Arete PROJECT
The obvious clean arete, sketchy high crux.

Charlie Barron climbing The Caveman

Shopping Cart Boulder

The new standard for hard bouldering in Billings. Named after the shopping cart found on the backside. Charlie Barron's love letter to Billings.

1. High Friction V7***

Stand start into a knee bar and then move out right to the obvious jug. Easier with a kneebar pad. Sketchy top out.

2. Super High Friction V8**

Sit start on an OK sloping crimp rail and climb into the start of High Friction. Toe hooky good times!

3. The Big Move PROJECT

Climb the proud arete. Bring your bouncy castle for the landing zone.

4. The Neanderthal PROJECT

Start on Super High Friction and link into The Caveman.

5. The Caveman V11****

Sit start on good rail, up to a left crimp, throw to a three finger pocket, then up left onto the crux face.

6. Ripple Your Nipple V8***

Around the left corner from the above climbs lies a clean prow. Left hand starts at the bottom of the arete and the right hand on a sidepull crimp just under the lip. Climb up the arete and face.

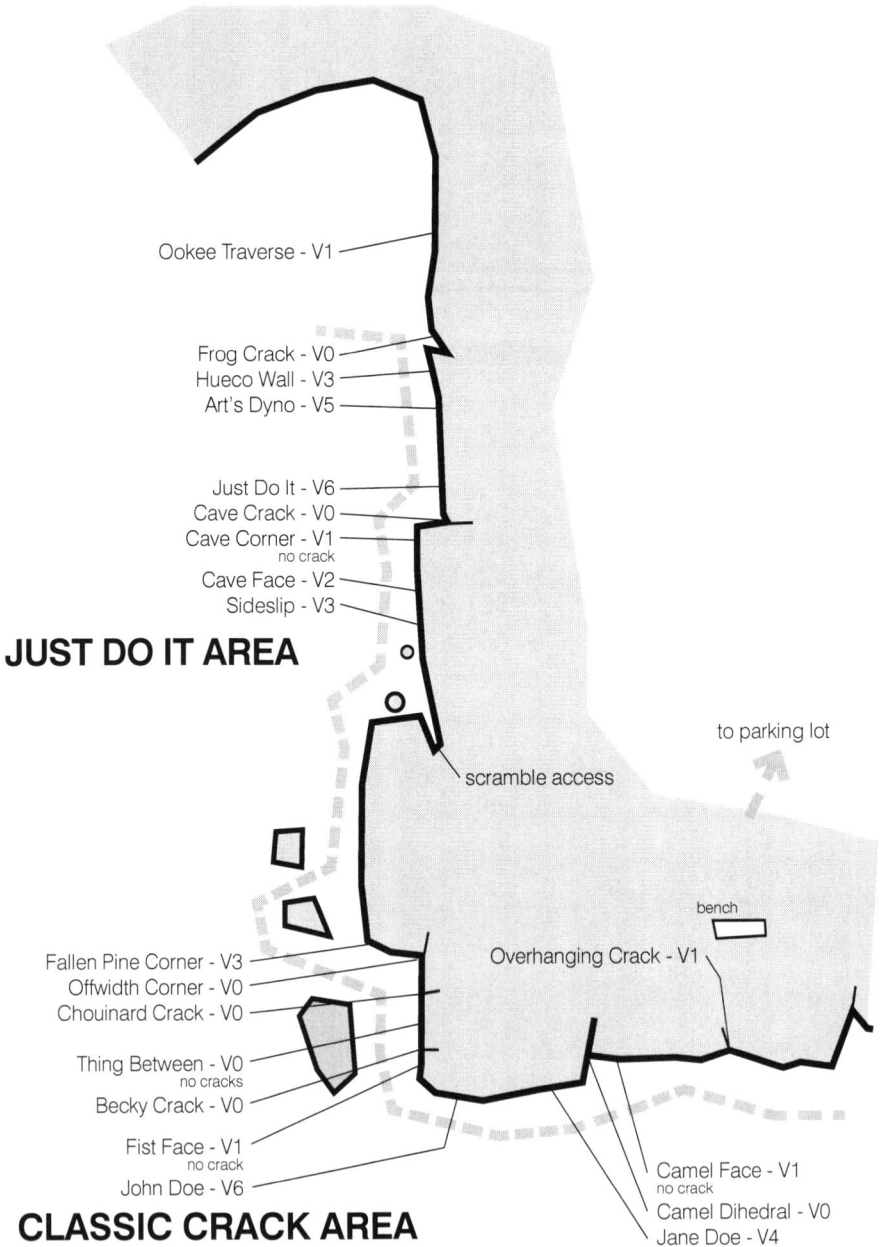

Ookee Traverse - V1

Frog Crack - V0
Hueco Wall - V3
Art's Dyno - V5

Just Do It - V6
Cave Crack - V0
Cave Corner - V1
no crack
Cave Face - V2
Sideslip - V3

JUST DO IT AREA

scramble access

to parking lot

bench

Fallen Pine Corner - V3
Offwidth Corner - V0
Chouinard Crack - V0

Overhanging Crack - V1

Thing Between - V0
no cracks
Becky Crack - V0

Fist Face - V1
no crack
John Doe - V6

Camel Face - V1
no crack

CLASSIC CRACK AREA

Camel Dihedral - V0
Jane Doe - V4

Zimmerman Park

Where

Take Highway 3 north out of town past the airport towards Lavina. After you pass the Zimmerman Trail turnoff there will be a parking lot on your left. Park here, the boulders lay directly south above the Rims.

Access

Zimmerman is a very popular park in Billings. Good behavior by climbers is always beneficial towards our stewardship of the sport. Keep your dog on a leash, pick up trash, and be friendly with inquisitors. Great mountain biking.

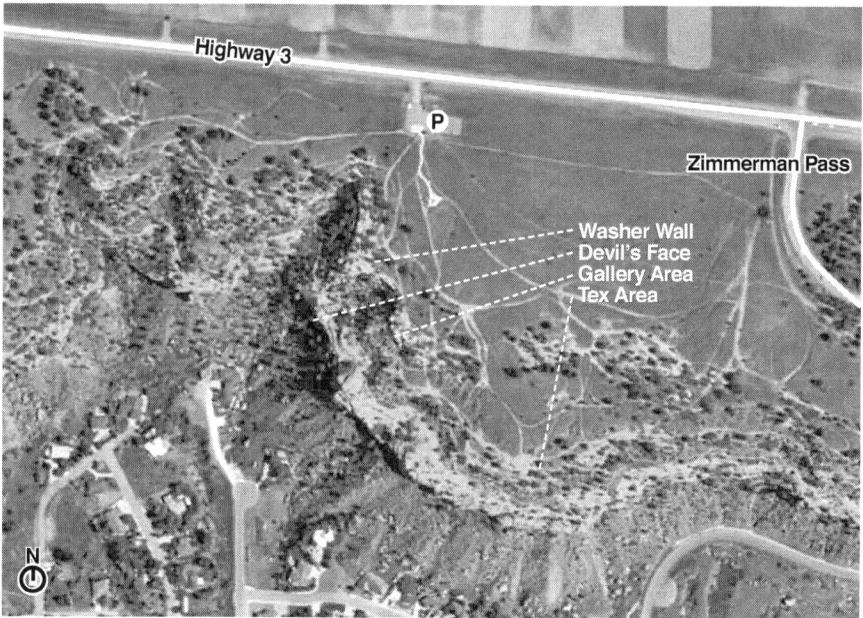

Highway 3

P

Zimmerman Pass

Washer Wall
Devil's Face
Gallery Area
Tex Area

N

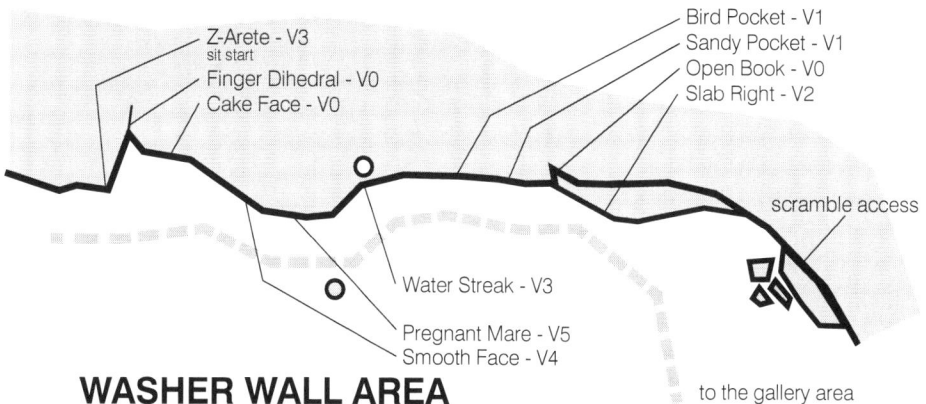

Z-Arete - V3
sit start
Finger Dihedral - V0
Cake Face - V0

Bird Pocket - V1
Sandy Pocket - V1
Open Book - V0
Slab Right - V2

scramble access

Water Streak - V3

Pregnant Mare - V5
Smooth Face - V4

WASHER WALL AREA

to the gallery area

Angela Douglas boulders up Tex

Beastly Dust Devil

Climb these boulder problems to defeat the Beastly Dust Devil in Zimmerman Park.

[ ] Sandy Pocket V0
[ ] Thing Between V0
[ ] Bird Pocket V1
[ ] `No Trow V1
[ ] Tex V2
[ ] Cave Face V2

[ ] Slab Right V2
[ ] Water Streak V3
[ ] Hueco Wall V3
[ ] I Owe Wyo V3
[ ] Smooth Face V4
[ ] Tex Traverse V4

Abominable Crack Man

The Abominable Crack Man is holding these crack climbs hostage, climb them to defeat him and set these lines free.

[ ] Beckey Crack V0
[ ] Chouinard Crack V0
[ ] Camel Dihedral V0
[ ] Finger Dihedral V0
[ ] Pine Cone Crack V0

[ ] Devils Face Left 5.9
[ ] Ogie Crack V1
[ ] Overhanging Crack V1
[ ] Sun Crack V2

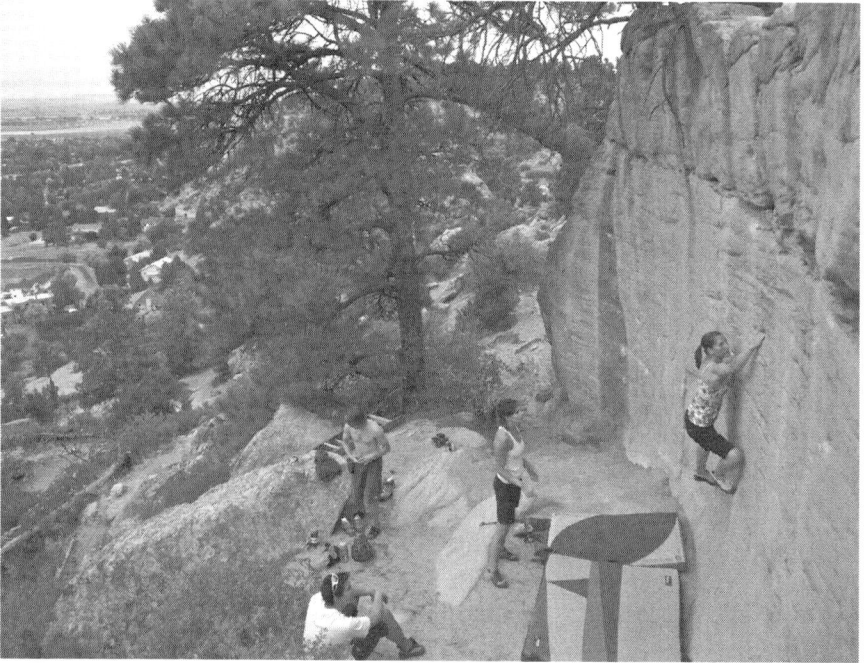

Lis Ten Harmsel climbs Bird Pocket on the classic Washer Wall

Aaron Ten Harmsel climbs Tex

Just Do It Area

1. Ookee Traverse V1*
The Ookee Wall features decent rock down low and horrible rock up high. Traverse the good band of rock on a great variety of holds. Look out for Poison Ivy. *(no photo)*

2. Frog Crack V0
Climb the flaring crack.

3. Hueco Wall V3*
Start two hands on a nice rail and move up through interesting pockets to a difficult top out, often dusty.

4. Art's Dyno V5*
One big graceful move. Start on the rail at about chest height and dyno to the even bigger rail high up.

PROJECT: Do Art's Dyno and climb straight up to the top.

5. Just Do It V6***
Stand start crimps and climb up through a shallow pocket and seam. The top out is not the crux but often dusty.

6. Just Do It Sit Start V7**
Sit start to Just Do It. Hard.

7. Cave Crack V1*
Start low in the crack and climb up through a slopey top out.

8. Cave Corner V1
Climb up the arete without using the crack.

9. Cave Face V2***
Start on small crimps, climb up to a nice lip, and mantle.

10. Sideslip V4**
Start on thin chips and move up the slab on more thin holds.

Classic Crack Area

1. Fallen Pine Corner V3
Start on the rail and climb up edges to a scary topout.

2. Offwidth Corner V0
Climb the crack in the corner, all holds on.

3. Chouinard Crack V0***
Climb the crack, all holds on.

4. Thing Between V1*
Climb the face between Becky Crack and Chouinard Crack without using the cracks.

5. Becky Crack V0**
Climb the crack all holds on.

6. Fist Face V1*
Climb up the face without using Becky Crack to the left.

Loren Rausch sending Just Do It (photo: Rausch collection)

Washer Wall Area

The next selection of boulder problems have tall finishes where falling is not a good idea. Thankfully most of the cruxes are down low and the finishes are slabby in nature. Anchors also exist above for those who want to drop a quick top rope.

1. Jane Doe V4
Start on pockets and climb up sandy holds.

2. Camel Dihedral V0*
Climb the crack.

3. Camel Face V1
Climb up the face right of the crack without using any of the crack.

4. Overhanging Crack V1***
Climb up through the bulge using the crack and face holds. One of the best of its grade in Billings.

5. Z-Arete V2*
Sit start on the overhanging nose and pull up onto the arête.

6. Finger Dihedral V0*
Climb the crack in the clean corner.

7. Cake Face V0
Climb up the shallow dihedral.

8. Smooth Face V4**
Climb into and through the amazing pocket.

9. Pregnant Mare V5*
Start on a fragile rail and pull up over the bulge.

Washer Wall Area
continued

1. Water Streak V3***
Start on the crack and a slopey pocket. Navigate crimps to the right and the crack to work your way up the slopey pod in the crack. A direct variation where you only use the crack for hands ups the grade to V4. Tall finish but the crack up high is only 5.9.

Many variations can be linked up on this wall. Below are some of the standards.

1. Slab Right V2* Start with one hand in a nice pocket and pull up to the slab finish. Exit left through the finish to Open Book. An easy version of Smooth Face.

2. Open Book V0* Start with one hand in the crack, with all holds on follow it to the finish.

3. Sandy Pocket V1 Start in the crack of Open Book, move left into chipped pockets, and up.

4. Bird Pocket V1* Start on a layback sidepull and climb up big moves through slopey pockets.

to Washer Wall

GALLERY AREA

Pine Cone Crack - V0
Sun Crack - V2
Left Arete - V1
I Owe Wyo - V3

Alpine Simulator - V0
chimney

scramble access

Ogie Crack - V1
Ponderosa
Crack - V0

PINE BOULDER

RHF Corner - V5
RHF Face - V3

Beach Slab - V0

Quarter Turn - V0

Fall of Man - V6

towards Tex and
walking access

Pine Boulder

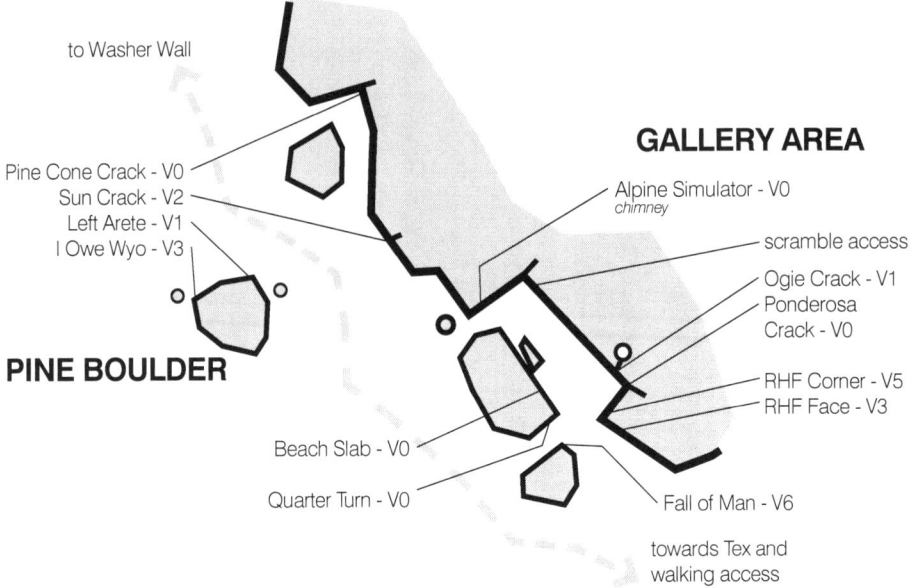

1. Left Arete V1*
Left hand starts on a hold on the arete and the right hand starts on a crimp on the overhanging face. Climb up the arete using only holds near the arete and on the overhanging face. Top out directly at the peak of the boulder.

2. I Owe Wyo V4*
Sit start on sharp crimps down low. Climb up crimps and slopers to the lip and then move up and left, topping out over the peak of the boulder. Using the cheater stone at the start makes it V3.

3. Right Arete V3**
Start the same as for the "I Owe Wyo" but this time skip the traverse and top out straight through the upper lip. Using the cheater stone at the start makes it V2.

4. Sun Crack V2***
Start in the underside of the crack.

1. Pine Cone Crack V0**
Sit start in the crack.

The Gallery

2. Alpine Simulator V0*
Pure squeeze chimney right of Beach Slab. *(no photo)*

3. Beach Slab V0*
Start on shallow dishes for your feet and hands. Continue up without using the left arete or the block on the right.

4. Quarter Turn V0**
Start on good holds down low inbetween the two boulders and climb up and onto the arete.

5. Ogie Crack V1**
Stand start using the thin finger crack. The tree on top has historically been considered fair game.

6. Ponderosa Crack V0*
Start low in the crack and climb up.

7. RHF Corner V5***
Start with your left hand on a crimp and right hand on the arete. Technical and balancy, sometimes sandy.

8. RHF Face V3*
Start on crimps. Messy landing zone.

9. Fall of Man V6**
Start on a crimp and sidepull and pull your way up the geometric block.

TEX AREA

to parking

easy scramble access

Stump - VB
Eagle Dihedral - V0

Tex - V2
sit start in crack

Greasy Pig - V3
direct start to tex

No Trow - V1
Big Trow - V3

towards the Gallery

towards Zimmerman Pass

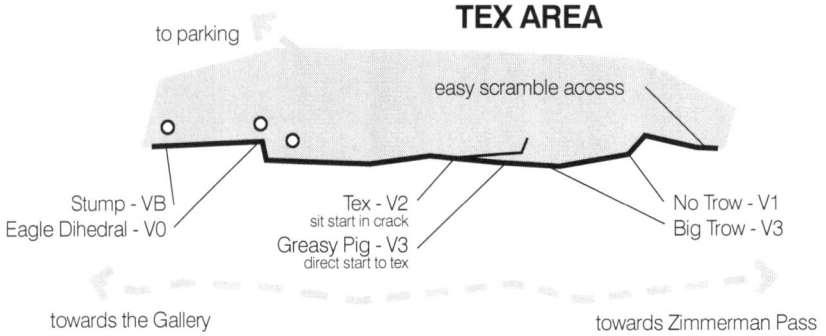

Eagle Graffiti Wall

1. Eagle Dihedral V1*
Stand start on dusty sloping ledges and move up through the corner.

2. Hole V0
Easy dusty face left of Eagle Dihedral. *(no photo)*

3. Durrrrrdy Roof V5
Because someone will ask. You've climbed better.

Tex Area

1. Tex V2****
Sit start in the crack and traverse up and right following the crack. Interestingly enough, not really a crack climb. One of the great boulder problems of Billings.

2. Greasy Pig V3***
Stand start on a positive side pull. Move out left from under the roof to a subtle crimp and finish on the upper half of Tex.

3. Big Trow V3*
Stand start on good crimps, throw high to more good crimps, and then top out.

4. Tex Traverse V4**
Start in a three finger pocket and traverse left into Tex. Pumpy good times.

5. No Trow V1*
Start on pockets and climb up through a unique pocket.

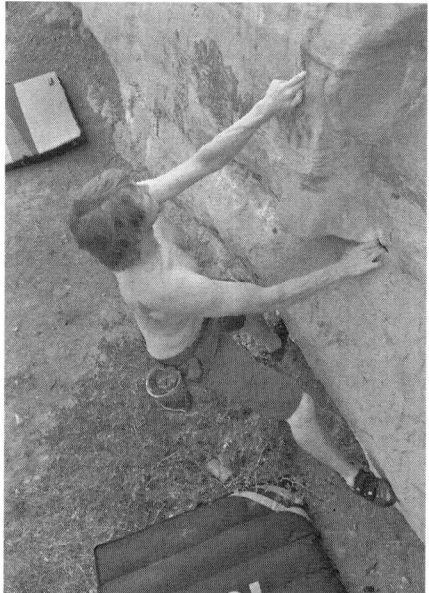

Miles Babcock climbs No Trow

The Devil's Face

To access the Devil's Face one must hike down the gully just below the Just Do It bouldering Area. As you descend, the wall will be on the skier's left. Look for the prominent horn / face that defines the top of the wall.

1. Devil's Crack Left 5.9**

An unusual crack bolted many years ago. The bolts only go two thirds of the way up, with the top section requiring some thin cams. No fixed anchors, use the trees above the Devils Head.

2. Devils Crack Right 5.10**

A fun crack line, the crux is thin but short. A couple bolts supplement the crack for gear. Fixed anchors at the top.

Shawn Gregory climbing underneath the Devils Face

Thad McGrail climbing Devils Crack Left

Waterfall Face

The Waterfall Face lies further south and east of the Devil's Face along the same cliff band. Both routes on this wall have good moderate movement but could use some more traffic to clean them up.

1. First Try 5.9**
Bolted sport climb with sport anchors.

2. Black and Blue 5.9**
Bolted sport climb with sport anchors.

With the right conditions an ice climb will form between the above two routes.

Shawn Gregory entering into the Fat Jawn

The Hidden Wall

The Hidden Wall lies further south and east of the Waterfall Face along the same cliff band. The routes need more traffic to clean them up a bit.

1. Texas Dreaming 5.9*

Climbs up through a couple huecos. Bolted sport climb.

3. Fat Jawn 5.7**

Bolted chimney. Interesting stemming and climbing with safely spaced bolts make this a great first lead climb for beginners.

What's the best route in town?

The one that doesn't crumble underneath you.

Most fascinating.

Phipps Park

Where
Take Rimrock Road west out of town follow the road as it turns north into Molt Road. After you cross under the train tracks look for a parking lot on your left. Park here. The boulders lay south near the butte. About a 5 minute hike in.

Access Notes
Phipps is a city park located outside city limits, (really). It also hosts a tournament grade disc golf course called Diamond X. Some of the holes weave through the boulders. Be on the lookout for flying discs. Despite frequent evidence of paintball, it is illegal to fire paintball guns in city parks.

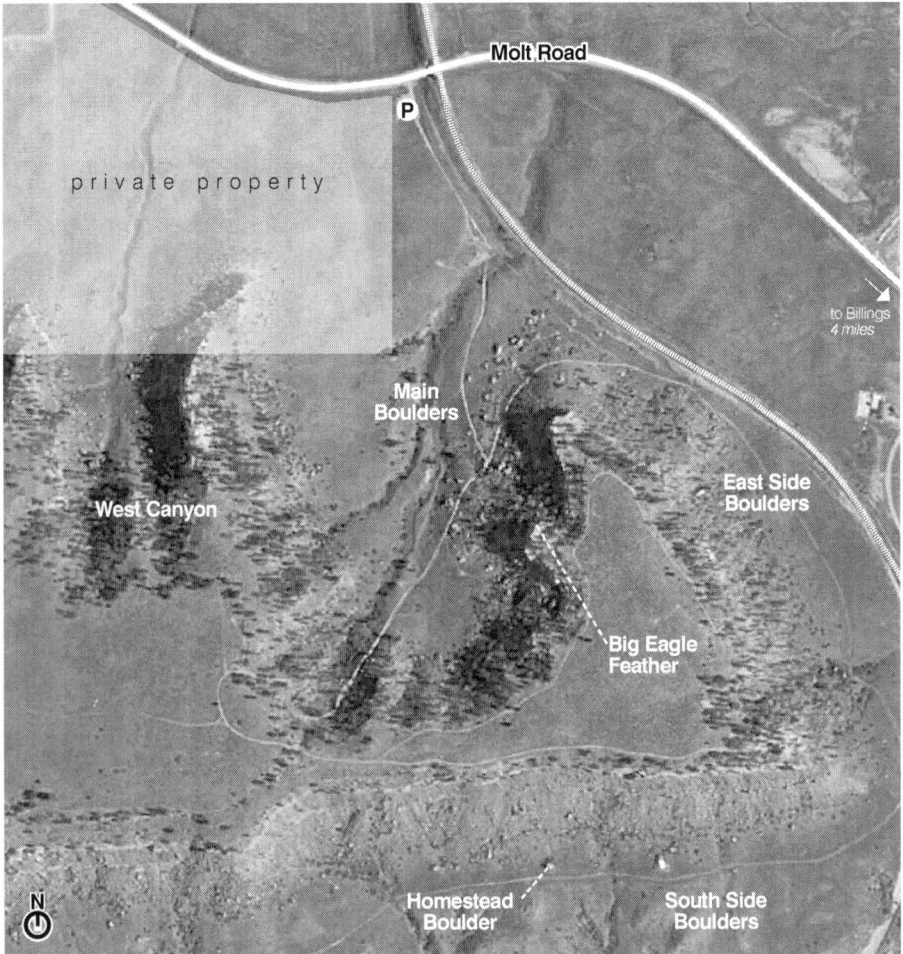

BUTTE

RAVINE

to Big Eagle Feather

The Breadloaf

Boxcar Boulder
Tall Boy

Hole Boulder

Tree Boulder

◄─ to eastside boulders

Fallen Boulder
Thigh Hooker

Main Boulder
Junior Boulder

First Hole

to parking lot ▼

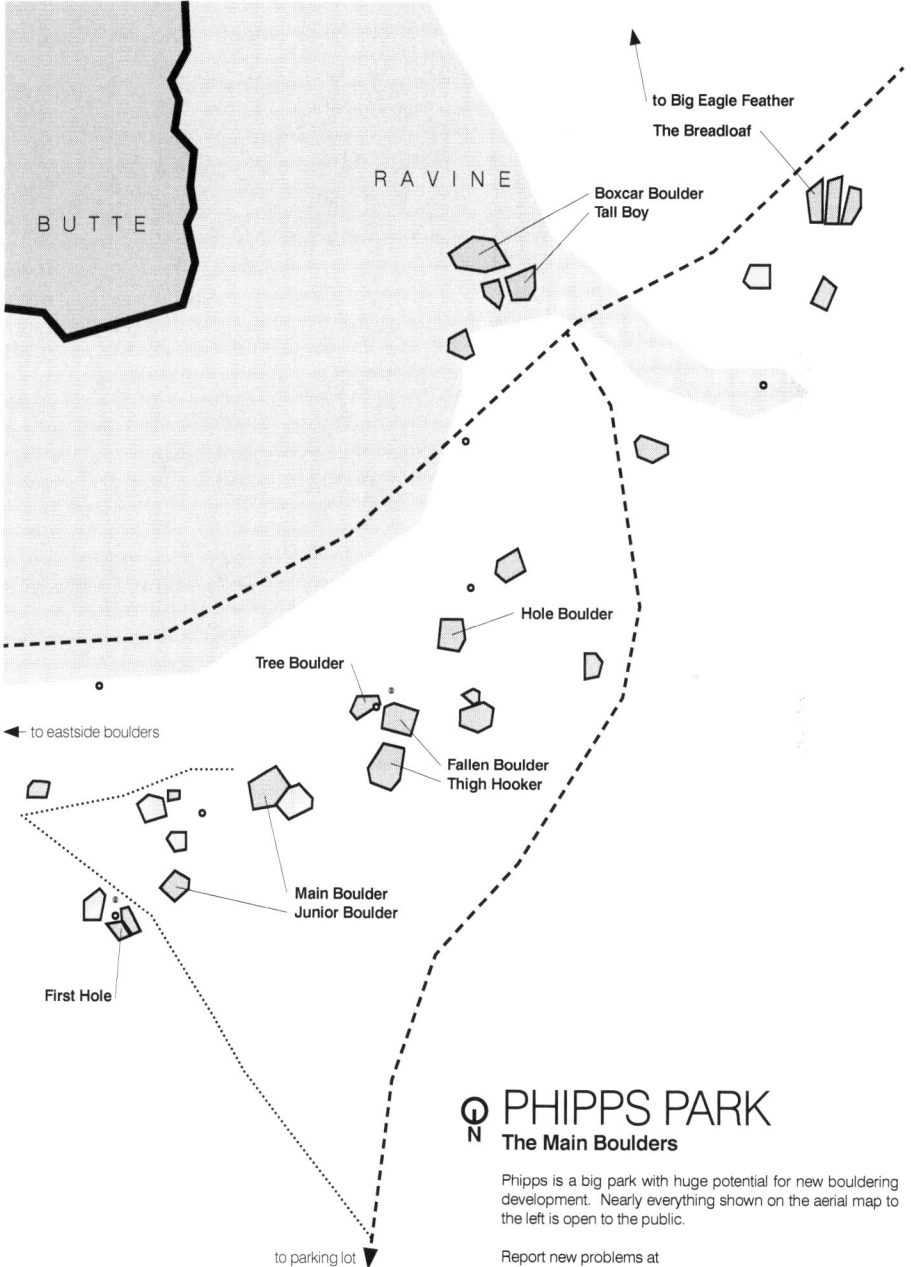

Ⓝ PHIPPS PARK
The Main Boulders

Phipps is a big park with huge potential for new bouldering development. Nearly everything shown on the aerial map to the left is open to the public.

Report new problems at
www.billingsclimbingguide.blogspot.com

Junior Boulders at Phipps

The First Hole Boulder, The Shorty Boulder, and the Tree Boulder are three boulders in the Main Boulders area at Phipps Park that are great for beginners and younger kids to get a feel for rock climbing and bouldering. The boulders are scaled down in size, have nice solid features, clean landings, and easy down climbs.

The best climbers start young and highlighting these boulders gives parents a chance to share the climbing experience with their kids.

First Hole Boulder

This boulder lies on the east side of the main boulder field, near the first hole of the disc golf course.

1. Metal Pancakes V0*

2. Crispy Corner V0**

3. Chimney Crickets V0
Climb the face right of the chimney, all holds on.

4. Cricket Wicket V0*
Climb the face right of the chimney, the left boulder is off.

5. Golfers and Folfers V1**
Climb the arete using the arete and small crimps on the right face.

6. Seam Dreams V1*
Climb the face.

Shorty Boulder

This boulder lies immediately west of the First Hole Boulder. Sit starts mandatory for the tall folks.

1. Bench Press V0*

Sit start on the sloping rail and press up to higher holds.

2. Tips and Toes V0

Start in the hole and climb up.

3. Wang Doodles V0**

Start on the good horn on the arete and move left and up.

4. Roc-a-saurus Rex V0**

Start on the good horn on the arete and move right and up.

5. Blank Face V0*

Climb the face on subtle holds

6. Sand Traps V0*

Connect the dots, climbing up the holes.

7. Dream Team Traverse V0***

Start in the right most hole of Sand Traps, traverse left, and finish on Bench Press. The top lip of the boulder is off.

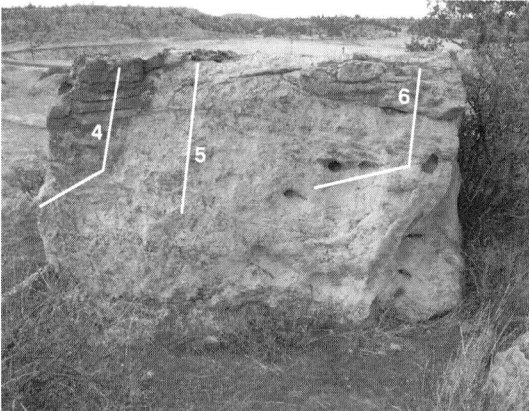

SloperZilla Junior

Climb these problems to win over SloperZilla Junior at Phipps Park

[ ] Crispy Corner V0
[ ] Cricket Wicket V0
[ ] Bench Press V0
[ ] Wang Doodles V0
[ ] Roc-a-saurus Rex V0

[ ] Dream Team Traverse V0
[ ] Trees R Us V0
[ ] The Flail Rail V1
[ ] Golfers and Folfers V1

Main Boulder
south face
Down climb: North side, a little sketchy for some, beginners should scope it out prior.

1. The Warm Up V0*
Start on dusty and fragile edges, climb up and left to large hollow pockets. Pull down, not out. The right start adds a grade.

2. Paintballer Personality Test V4*
Start on thin crimps pull two moves and finish on the jugs of the Warm-Up.

3. Dustin and Greg V1*
Skip the technical start of Paintballer Personality Test by using a running jump start to the good holds.

4. Piton Scar V1**
Stand start using the pocket and climb straight up. Using the good holds up and right make things slightly easier

Main Boulder
continued

5. Phipps Arete V2***
Stand start on crimps, climb up on more crimps. Beautiful line.

6. Cube Slab V3**
Stand start on crimps near the center of the west face. Climb and mantle up the slab without using the left or right arete.

7. The Left Arete V1*
Stand start using crimps and the arete. Climb up the arete left of Cube Slab.

8. North Warm Up V0
Climb the arete and crack.

9. The Seamstress V1**
Start on sloping edges down low and move right and up using holds on or near the seam.

10. Fatal Flakes V0
Navigate questionable underclings and flakes.

11. Grand Poohbah PROJECT**
Find a way up the obtuse corner of the north arete. Bring lots of pads.

Thigh Hooker Boulder

This boulder lies immediately west of the Main Boulder.

1. Thigh Hooker V0*
Multiple start variations lead up the arete and into the unique thigh hook move. Sandy.

2. North Face V0
Multiple variations. Also the down climb.

3. Mini-Cave V5**
Start low down in the mini cave on nice crimps and climb up through the steep section, avoiding the boulder immediately behind you, and top out. Not dabbing tends to be the crux.

4. Rattler Roof V1**
Technically the finishing moves to Mini-Cave. Start on pockets at the lip of the overhang and pull over.

5. Failed Love Date V2***
Start the same as Mini-Cave but move left and up the large pockets to the slopey and sandy finish.

6. Long & Winding Road V3**
Start the same as for Mini-Cave but move left, and keep traversing left til you top out on Thigh Hooker.

7. North Arete V2*
Climb pockets and the arete, little dusty up high.

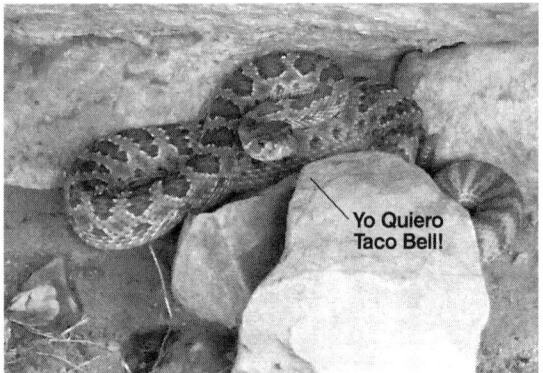

Yo Quiero Taco Bell!

Rudy the Rattler wants to party with you!

Fallen Boulder

Fresh! One morning in 2005? this boulder just appeared after falling from above.

1. Slapstick Traverse V4****

AKA The Sloper Traverse. Sit start down low on the north west edge of the boulder and traverse right gradually up on slopers. Turn the corner and mantle up to finish. Pumpy!

2. Belly slap Mantle V2*

Start the same as the Slapstick Traverse but instead directly mantle up and out.

3. Going the Distance V4*

Start the same as the Slapstick Traverse but at the finish continue right traversing the upper edge of the boulder till you get back to the start.

4. Patina Wall V0

Start on positive little glassy features near the center of the face and climb to the top.

5. Mantle Skillz V3***

Start on the sloping upper edge of the boulder. Move out right and mantle up. Sit down start???

6. Throw Your Hands Up V5***

Stand start in a pinchy pocket and huck up for the l.

7. The Gun Show V9**

Start on Mantle Skills and roll into the pockets of Throw Your Hands Up finish on the big throw.

Kyle Clark riding the Slapstick Traverse (photo: Anna Biegel)

Tree Boulder

A great boulder for kids, this boulder is easy to find with the large tree growing in the side.

1. Soft Hang V0

On the northeast side of the boulder is a slight vertical seam. Start on the soft sloping ledge. (no photo)

2. The Flail Rail V1**

Sit start in the shallow crack at the arete and climb up.

3. Trees R Us V0**

Climb the arete avoiding the tree.

4. Mini Huecos V0*

Sit start in the holes and climb up.

5. Rocks are People Too V0

Climb the face.

Mike Fallon on Phipps Arete

Hole Boulder

This boulder lies immediately west of the Fallen Boulder signified by the hole pocket on its east face. Descent is best to down climb the Warm Up Arete.

1. Mantle Warmup V0
Start on the arete and move left on good holds and mantle up.

2. Warm Up Arete V0*
Start left hand on a side pull and right hand on a jug undercling down low.

3. Sloper Skills Pay Bills V2**
Sit start right hand in a slightly positive pocket and the left hand in a juggy pocket and move up the sloping ramp.

4. Fingery Thing V1*
Start in the big undercling, move up and right to the sloping edge, and top out.

5. Hard Pressed V3**
Sit start on the nice ledge low on the corner and mantle up to sloping edges and top out.

6. The Stab V6*
Left hand on the arete and right hand in a small pocket, then stick the good pocket, and finish on Phippsin" Around.

7. Phippsin' Around V1***
Right hand stand start on the nice edge and climb up through pockets and ledges.

8. Phippsin' Around Sit Start V4*
Lower start with your left hand in a small pocket and your right hand on a small crimp.

9. King Corner V0*
Juggy holds and pockets on the little arete on the north face.

Tall Boy

This boulder lies above and west of the main boulders in a small basin.

1. Lickin' Lichen V0*
Climb the north face, easy but tall.

2. Pillow Dreams V0*
climb the northwest arete.

Boxcar Boulder

West Face

This long rectangular boulder lies immediately south of Tall Boy.

1. Two Holes to Heaven V3**
Climb the left face up into the pockets and throw for the top. Bring pads and a great spotter.

2. Space Race Arete V1**
Climb the arete.

Boxcar Boulder
north face

2. Space Race Arete V1**
Climb the arete.

3. Big Freaking Reach V1*
Climb the face left of the arete. The arete is off. Reachy.

4. Pocket Protector V0*
Climb the face connecting pockets

5. Chipped Route
Cool climbers don't chip routes.

Shawn Gregory on Space Race Arete

Boxcar South
Uphill side of the Boxcar Boulder

6. West End Bend V0***
Unique juggy pockets create endless opportunities for traverses. A little dusty, needs more traffic in its hidden location.

Kyle Clark boldly steps into Space Race Arete

Mike Fallon on Rattler Roof

Shawn Gregory crimping down on Failed Love Date

Anna Biegel testing out Pocket Protector

Forrest Murter tops out Cube Slab

Joel displaying some Mantle Skillz (photo Anna Biegel)

SloperZilla - climb these for victory

[ ] West End Bend V0
[ ] Thigh Hooker V0
[ ] Piton Scar V1
[ ] Phippsin' Around V1
[ ] Phipps Arete V2
[ ] Sloper Skills Pay Bills V2
[ ] Sage Operator V2

[ ] Cube Slab V3
[ ] Long & Winding Road V3
[ ] Outer Edge of Time V3
[ ] Mantle Skillz V3
[ ] Hard Pressed V3
[ ] Slapstick Traverse V4
[ ] The Seam V4

The Breadloaf

Easily recognizable, also known as the Three Kings, or the Split Boulder.

1. West Bread Crack V0
Climb the obvious crack, tall and dirty.

2. Ryan's Sloper Traverse V8**
On the north face start on the nice corner and traverse up to the high point and top out.

3. The Smooth and the Sharp V5*
Start on the sloper and use the neighboring boulder for your feet and traverse the lip of the boulder topping out at the high point.

4. The Outer Edge of Time V3***
Sit start low in the crack on the good edge on the left side of the crack, then climb up the left arete using the edges of the crack and face holds out left.

Eastside Boulders

The following boulders lie up the hill and to the east of the prominent butte. Following the foot trail will take you right next to the Leaning Boulder. The Arrowhead boulder is a couple minutes hike further south. Many boulders lay waiting for more development.

Charlie Barron on Red Russian

Leaning Boulder

As you hike east and south from the main boulders this will be the first quality boulder you come to.

1. Red Russian V5**

Start on a left crimp and the right corner, climb up the face. The block below is off after you start.

2. Little Russkie V1*

Climb Red Russian but the block below is on for feet.

3. Tom Cruise V7

Start low on the easy northwest face, climb up on good holds, then drop down into the start of Red Russian.

Arrowhead Boulder

From the Leaning Boulder, hike further south on the trail. Can't miss it.

1. Arrow Slab V1
Climb the slab. Would benefit from more cleaning.

2. Loper Sloper V2**
Sit start low, work into bear hugging the boulder's aretes and climb up.

Hidden Boulder

An example of what's found further south in Phipps Park. South of the Leaning Boulder, up in a draw and concealed by a tree, lies this boulder and many others, waiting for some cleaning.

Southside Boulders

The following boulders lie on the southside of the primary butte. These are really just a sampling, many more are waiting for development. From the parking lot, hike south, and left (east) around the butte on a well worn trail. The hike takes about 10-15 minutes.

Sagebrush Boulder

One of the first large boulders you come to as you hike around the southeast corner of the butte. From this boulder you should be able to see the cattle shack and the Homestead Boulder to the west.

1. Southside Warm Up V0* Climb the pocketed face.

2. Sage Operator V2*** Start low on the lip, traversing up and left thru delicate balance moves.

3. Wagon Wheel Water Slide V0** Starting from the southeast bush, climb the slab.

Seam Boulder

This boulder sits to the west of the cattle shack just up the hill.

1. The Seam V4***
Sit start low in the crack and climb up using the seam and other holds. Steep and powerful. Great problem for the V4 climber.

Concrete Boulder

This boulder sits just down the hill and west of the Seam Boulder.

1. South Beach V0*
Climb the face.

2. Aggregate Dreams V2**
Sit start on the arete and climb up the face and arete.

Hey Jim, I see you shaved!

Yes, and I see you've grown the prerequisite Montana Mountain Man facial hair

It keeps me warm in the winter and its low maintenance

You must not climb in Billings, I shaved my beard because I was combing sand out of it all day

Climbing on the Homestead Boulder

Homestead Boulder

A very large cubical boulder west of the cattle shack. Unfortunately only two sides host quality rock. Big moves, high cruxes, multiple pads recommended.

1. Ranch Traverse V5**** Start on the southeast edge of the good rock in a small pocket. Traverse left through pockets, turn the corner, traverse through a thin section, turn the corner again, and finish.

2. Big Star V6*** Climb up through slopers and pockets to the airy crux. Reachy and sketchy.

3. Spur Kicking V4**** Climb the arete up pockets to a reachy move. It's a hand foot match high off the deck for the shorter climbers.

4. PROJECT
Climb the west face without using the arete.

5. Homestead Arete V1*
Climb the arete. Has great potential, but more rock needs to be cleaned up high.

6. Down Climb V0*
Climb down (or up) the deep huecos and flakes.

Kaleb Loper climbing Homestead Arete

Phipps Rope Routes

The buttes above Phipps hold the usual mix of good rock and bad rock. Most development has been with the many crack climbs. Only one is listed here.

1. Big Eagle Feather 5.11b****

The greatest crack climb in Montana. A big statement, but one that's hard to argue.

Located in a prow above and slightly west of the Boxcar Boulder. It is sometimes hidden behind the lone pine tree next to it.

Start right off the deck into a roof and then 40 feet of splitter hands to thin hands. A two bolt anchor lies immediately at the top of the crack. If you want to top rope you'll need to create your own anchor above, long webbing recommended.

Justin Willis leading Big Eagle Feather

Gregory Hills

History

Gregory Hills has been the prime rope climbing location on the rims since before the housing lots were developed. Back then it was called the "Horse Pasture" due to the area below the routes literally being pasture. Up until 2006 there was also great bouldering at the cul-de-sac below the Walkup. First ascent history has since been lost due to the transient nature of the climbers in the region, but a few people have been crucial to the development of the area. Brian Hagerty, who's been climbing around Billings since the early 80's, put together the first known guide to the area in 1991 and sold it via photocopy for $1. This public knowledge centralized climber traffic and helped Gregory Hills become the hub of Billings climbing. Brian also keeps route beta current on mountainproject.com and was my climbing partner and tour guide when I first moved to town in 2004. In 2001, Ari Greenberg and Jim Rott updated the area by adding bolt anchors to the more popular climbs and bolting some of the better face climbs like Prime Rib, Faster Pussycat, and Rockchuck Arete.

Where

From downtown, take Rimrock Road west. Turn right onto Gregory Hills Drive and head up the hill. Take a right onto Rockwood Circle. Park on the street and avoid bloking driveways. Hike the trail going up and left towards the rims. The first climb you will encounter is Bumblie with a Drill, see page 100. You will be hiking east to west along the base of the rims, but to logically organize the climbs like they are geographically located I have listed them going west to east.

Style & Anchors

Due to the nature of the rock, top roping is the common practice at Gregory Hills. Many climbs have anchors at the top. To get to the top of the rims without having to put on a harness you have a couple options. You can either hike to the west end of the cliff band to a scramble gully, climb the chimney just west of the route Center Face, or free solo the 5.4 route The Walkup. Your other option is to lead a sport or trad route to the top. After each climbs' description I've listed whether the route is generally climbed via sport, trad, or top rope, and what the anchor situation is like at the top of the route.

Please note that because of the soft rock, top rope anchors should extend over the edge to keep the rope from sawing cuts into the rock. Routes like Barney Rubble are showing considerable scars.

If you are interested in route development, the longer the bolts the better. Expansion bolts are often not the optimal solution, glue-ins have been more successful in some of the softer rock. Be suspect and test every anchor..

Access

Gregory Hills climbing is on city parkland above million dollar homes. Avoid unnecessary yelling, the whole neighborhood can hear you. The rims east of Rockwood Circle sits just outside the park boundary above an unsympathetic house owner, do not climb in that area.

Kaleb Loper leading Prime Rib

Scramble Access
The Walkup
Barney Rubble

Gregory Drive

P

Gregory Drive

Gregory Drive

Sycamore Lane

Rockwood Circle

Gregory Drive

Gregory Drive

N

Rimrock Road

Looking up the easiest access to the top of the rims at Gregory Hills. The gully is located at the far western point of the climbing, just around the corner from Cliffs of Insanity. The rock is relatively clean, low angle, and not exposed, but good shoes are recommended.

Ian McCracken climbs the bulbous features of Cliffs of Insanity

CLIFFS OF INSANITY AREA

1. Cliffs of Insanity 9+****
Interesting climbing up steep slopey pockets and bulges. Sport climb, bolts for anchors.

2. Inconceivable 5.10c*
The left most line on the face starts in a small pocket and climbs up holds left of Cliffs of Insanity. Top Rope, use the anchors on Cliffs of Insanity.

3. Human Alien Being 5.10d*
Climb the pockets right of Cliffs of Insanity to a cruxy mantel. Tope Rope, use Cliffs of insanity anchor and make a directional.

Tanner Callendar on a well earned lead of The Bishop.

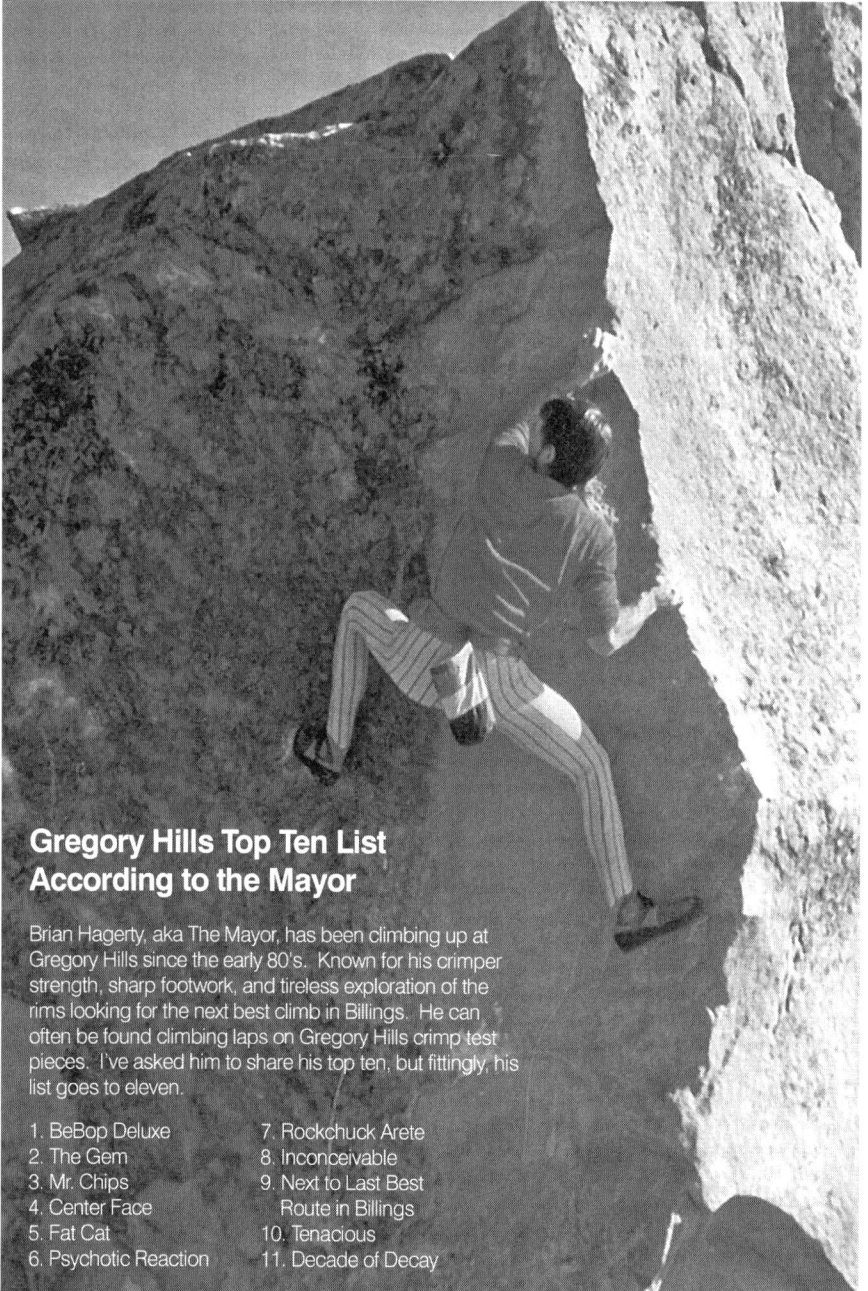

Gregory Hills Top Ten List
According to the Mayor

Brian Hagerty, aka The Mayor, has been climbing up at Gregory Hills since the early 80's. Known for his crimper strength, sharp footwork, and tireless exploration of the rims looking for the next best climb in Billings. He can often be found climbing laps on Gregory Hills crimp test pieces. I've asked him to share his top ten, but fittingly, his list goes to eleven.

1. BeBop Deluxe
2. The Gem
3. Mr. Chips
4. Center Face
5. Fat Cat
6. Psychotic Reaction
7. Rockchuck Arete
8. Inconceivable
9. Next to Last Best Route in Billings
10. Tenacious
11. Decade of Decay

Brian Hagerty, circa 1986, climbing the now demolished Carter's Number at the base of Gregory Hills (photo: Hagerty collection)

NASTY VICAR AREA

1. Arete PROJECT
Thin holds on an arete.

2. Chipped Route

3. Nasty Vicar 5.10b***
Climb up the hand crack and venture left into a thin crack, climbing it to the top. Trad climb, gear (may be difficult), tree anchor.

4. The Bishop 5.10a***
Climb the start of Nasty Vicar, exiting onto face holds and a big undercling out right when the crack gets thin. Trad climb, bolt, questionable crack gear, bolts for anchors,

5. Chimney 5.8*
The wider crack right of The Bishop. No fixed Gear.

Chad Chadwick climbing on the Rims in 1967 (photo: Chadwick collection)

NASTY VICAR AREA

1. Punks on the Rims 5.10a
Top Rope. No fixed gear.

2. Brown Sugar 5.11a**
Climb the face up into the sea of swiss cheese pockets and finish on some power crimp moves. Sport climb, bolts for anchors..

3. Arete PROJECT

Crack-a-saurus
Climb these crack climbs at Gregory Hills to defeat Crackasaurus

[ ] Mountaineers Route 5.6
[ ] Barney Rubble Left 5.7
[ ] Welcome to Billings 5.8
[ ] Roof Right 5.8
[ ] Sapsucker 5.9
[ ] Easy Street 5.9

[ ] Barney Rubble 5.9
[ ] Reuben 5.9
[ ] Elephant Slipper 5.10
[ ] Nasty Vicar 5.10
[ ] Black Crack 5.10+
[ ] Excuse Abuse 5.11

EASY STREET AREA

1. Dirty Shower 5.11a
Climb the arete with decent rock down low into sandy holds up high. Top Rope, eyebolts for anchors.

2. Easy Street 5.9**
Climb the left angling crack with a unique crux move at the slopey bulge in the middle. Top Rope, eyebolts for anchors.

3. Love it to Death 5.11c*
Climb the face just right of Easy Street aiming for the unique bulges up high. Top Rope, eyebolts for anchors.

4. Conspiracy Theory 5.12b*
Climb the face left of Assassin up to a bulge that is shared by Assassin and then exit up left. Top Rope, tree for anchors.

5. Assassin 5.11a***
Climb the thin seam left of Billings Radio on technical and balancy moves. Sport climb, bolts for anchors.

EASY STREET AREA

6. Ringling 5.8*
The crack system left of Billings Radio. Top rope, make your own anchors.

7. Billings Radio 5.11d****
Climb the attached pillar up nice crimps and sidepulls to a crux finish. Top rope, chains for anchors, difficult anchors to access, use caution.

8. Funhouse 5.11b*
Climb up nice easy huecos to a slabby crux top out. Top rope, make your own anchor.

CrimperStein
Climb these face climbs to defeat CrimperStein

[ ] Prime Rib 5.9
[ ] Tree Route 5.10a
[ ] Cliffs of Insanity 5.10a
[ ] Peanut Brittle 5.10d
[ ] Center Face 5.11a
[ ] Faster Pussycat 5.11a

[ ] Assassin 5.11a
[ ] Rockchuck Arete 5.11b
[ ] Psychotic Reaction 5.11b
[ ] Brown Sugar 5.11b
[ ] Billings Radio 5.11d
[ ] Reubens Brother 5.11d

EASY STREET AREA

1. The Gem 5.11c****
Climb the corner using small holds and seams on some of the best rock at Gregory Hills.
Top rope, bolt anchors.

2. Psychotic Reaction 5.11b/c****
Very unique climbing on the jutting blade of rock. Start up the corner left of the prow, after 10-15 feet climb up onto the blade and climb that to the top. Top Rope, make your own anchors.

Do you like my new glasses?

They're ridiculously enormous.
What 80's sitcom are you from?

They keep sand out of my eyes while climbing.
Plus they make my face look smaller!

Seriously.
You're the mother from Who's the Boss?
Growing Pains?
Family Ties?

REUBEN AREA

1. Decade of Decay 5.10d**
Climb up the pocketed face with the crux at the top. Top rope, bolts for anchors.

2. Flakes A Lot 5.11d*
Start left of Reuben on flakes climbing up towards the crux at the overhanging flake. Somewhat reachy. Top rope, bolts for anchors.

3. Reuben 5.9***
A nice crack corner. Slightly more difficult than Welcome to Billings. Trad climb, bolts for anchors.

4. Reuben's Brother 5.11d***
Start either in the dirty corner or climb the slabby but cleaner prow. The top half (crux) has cool pockets and much better rock than below. Top rope, bolts for anchors.

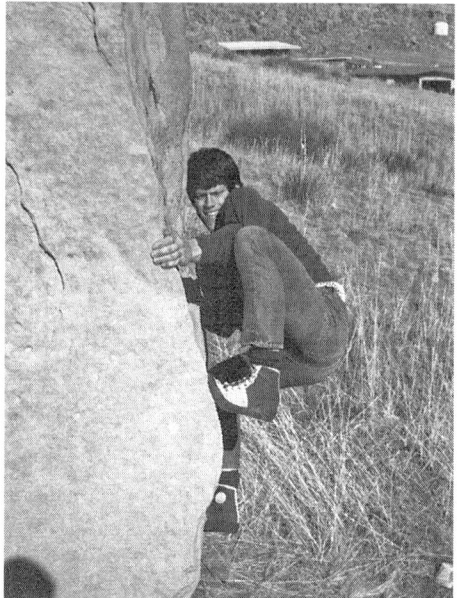

Chad Chadwick bouldering before it was cool and the housing developments moved in. (photo: Chadwick collection)

FULL SAIL AREA

1. Fat Cat 5.11d****
Climb the bottom of Faster Pussycat. After the mini roof traverse left and take on the steep face. The direct start was climbed, then holds broke, and is now an open project (The Cat's Meow). Sport climb, bolts for anchors.

2. Faster Pussycat 5.11a/b****
Start in friendly finger crack, navigate the mini roof, then climb up thin crimps to the steep layback crack finish. Classic. Leadable with gear and bolts, bolts for anchors.

3. Rockchuck Arete 5.11b****
Climb slopey crimps up into the arete 20 feet from the top. Tackle the arete from both sides. Technical, unique, and super fun. Sport climb, bolts for anchors.

4. Peanut Brittle 5.10d**
Climb the face between Rockchuck Arete and Full Sail. This climb finishes on a small ledge 10' below the top. Top rope, bolts for anchors.

5. Full Sail 5.12a
Used to be the ultra classic crack climb of Gregory Hills, might still be. In 2010 a block section of the crux thin hands section slid (settled?) a couple inches. It's been climbed since then, but beware. A steep layback crack system will take you to a decent rest before the steeper thin hands section exits you up right. Bolts for anchors.

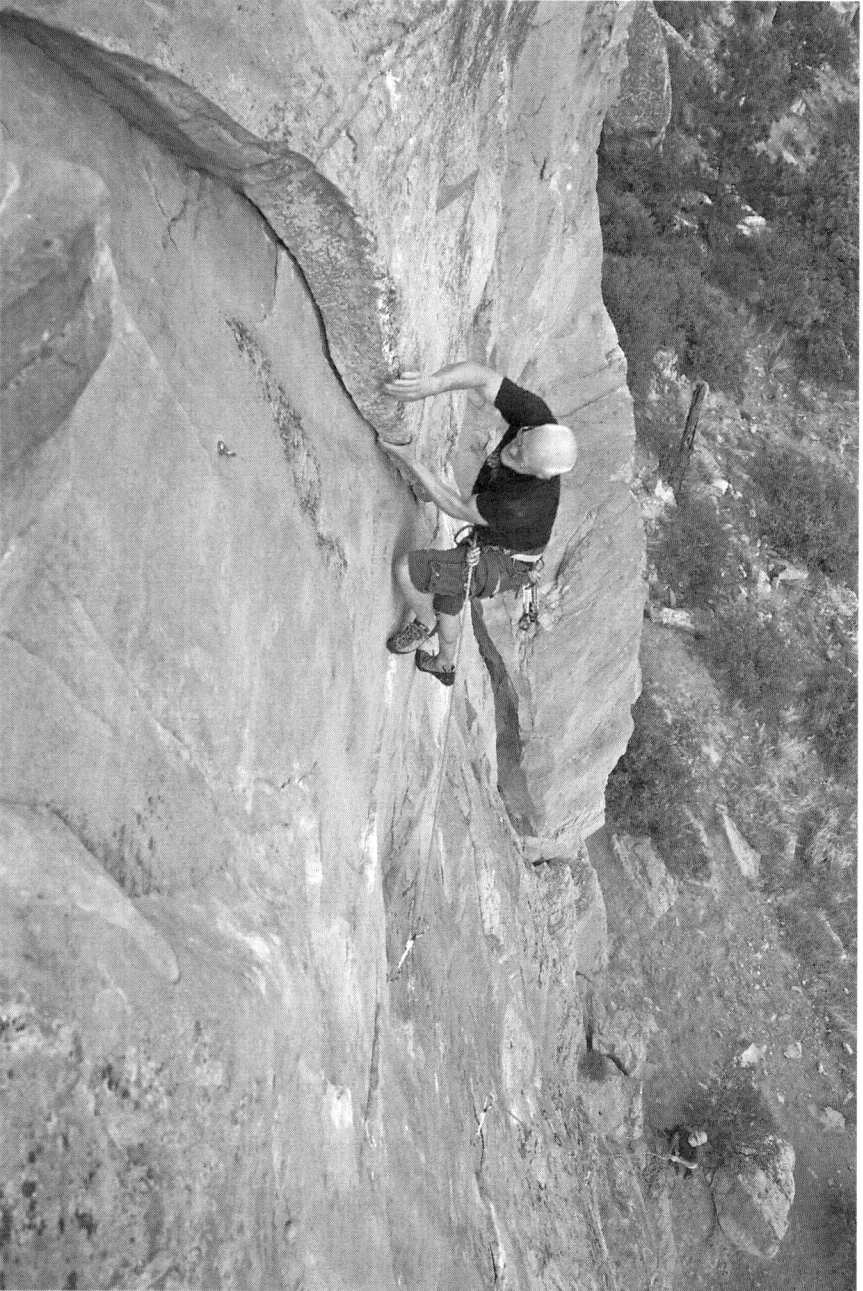

Jim Rott climbing Faster Pussycat.

CENTER FACE AREA

1. The Chasm 5.5
The obvious deep slot chimney left of the Center Face area that can be used for access to the top. Make your own anchor. *(no photo)*

2. Mr. Chips 5.12c****
One of the great crimper lines of Gregory Hills. Start in a small gully, avoiding the cheater rock behind you. Climb thin holds into the nice sharp black stained rock. Top rope, make your own anchors.

3. New Age 5.12c**
Similar style of climbing to Mr. Chips with some longer reaches. Top rope, make your own anchors.

4. BeBop Deluxe 5.12a****
Fun sustained climbing up typical Rimrock crimps, seams, and pockets. Move left when you get to the bulge. Be sure to top out to earn the full grade. Top rope, bolts for anchors.

5. Shark Sandwich 5.12a*
A variation of BeBop Deluxe tucked next to Center Face. Start right of BeBop Deluxe and avoid all Center Face holds. Midway up, share a couple moves with BeBop, then take a direct line to the top, avoiding the temptation to bail onto Center Face. Top rope, use anchor bolts on Center Face for anchors.

6. Center Face 5.11a***
See next page.

CENTER FACE AREA

6. Center Face 5.11a***
Start up into the boxy crack, through some slopey bulges, and finish navigating the final seam. A great sporty face climb. Sport climb and popular top rope, bolts for anchor.

7. Right Face 5.11c
Climb up into the obvious manufactured pocket chipped into the black face and then finish on less intensive climbing. Top rope, make your own anchors.

8. The Mayor 5.11b*
Start in the crack and halfway up move onto the face. Top rope, make your own anchors.

9. Dragonfly 5.10d*
Connect the huecos while staying right of the crack. Big crux move at the top. Route has potential, just needs more traffic to clean it up. Top rope, make your own anchors.

10. Saint Bridget's Cross 5.11d*
Start climbing through a couple of huecos, then traverse right around the corner and solve the steep finish onto a slab. Top rope, make your own anchors.

Justin Willis leading Elephant's Memory

 Yup.

Space, eh?

 Yeah

Sounds extreme

As extreme as climbing 10
feet above a TCU in rimrock?

 Yup

You're so dreamy

THE WALKUP AREA

1. St. Brigid's Cross 5.11c*
Top rope, make your own anchors.

2. Elephant Slipper 5.10b****   Elephant's Memory 5.10d***
Nice hand to finger crack. "Slipper" goes left at the slot, while "Memory" goes straight up. Trad climb, bolts for anchors.

3. Chipped Route 5.11a
Ethics of bygone years have given us this wall of drilled pockets in lousy rock. This practice is unacceptable today. The route is becoming increasingly difficult as holds break or fall off. Tope rope, bolts for anchors.

4. Pickpocket 5.11a*
Climb the water streak left of the Walkup. If you're on good holds you've wandered too far right. Top rope, bolts for anchors.

5. The Horse Pasture 5.7**
Climb the face left of the Walkup without using any part of the crack. Top rope, bolts for anchors.

6. Walkup 5.5***
The best and most popular beginner climb at Gregory Hills. Named because the route is often soloed to access the top of the rims for top rope setup. The right exit is the more difficult of the two. Pigeons occasionally can be found in the crack near the top. Trad climb, bolts for anchors.

THE WALKUP AREA

1. The Gauntlet PROJECT
Overhanging face with thin pockets. The holds are there, just needs to be climbed. Top rope, make your own anchors.

2. Tenacious 5.12b*
Climb the start of Welcome to Billings to the undercling flake and then up the face on pockets and crimps. Top rope, bolts for anchors.

3. Welcome to Billings 5.8+****
Named for the likelyhood of being a climbers first climb in Billings. A flaring finger crack with footholds and stemming that rewards good technique. A good crack that sees a lot of traffic has given this route some of the best rock in Billings. A fun safe lead climb. Trad climb, bolts for anchors.

4. The Girl Inbetween 5.12a*
Climb the face between Welcome to Billings and the Tree Route. Both cracks are off route. Interesting wandering route finding. Top rope, bolts for anchors.

THE WALKUP AREA

4. The Girl Inbetween 5.12a**
Climb the face between Welcome to Billings and the Tree Route. Both cracks are off route. Interesting wandering route finding. Top rope, bolts for anchors.

5. Tree Route 5.10a***
It may be a crack but it climbs like a face. Start on big moves in a steep crack aiming for some juicy huecos. A good rest and easier climbing takes you to the technical crux near the top. The "direct start" is 11a/b. Sport climb, bolts for anchors.

6. It's All There 5.12a
Do the Tree Route start, once you reach the big huecos climb the face and pockets without using the crack. Big moves or dyno at the top. Top rope, use the anchors of the Tree Route.

mmmm.... crack climbing!

bah! bouldering is so much more evolved

but you can't even climb a 5.8 crack

my shoes are too tight

Chris Guyer rope soloing Welcome to Billings

BARNEY RUBBLE AREA

1. Black Crack 5.10***
A proud and intimidating crack climb west of the Barney Rubble Area. Climb a steep and clean crack into the flaring off width roof finish. A true route for the true trad climber. Trad climb, bolts for anchors.

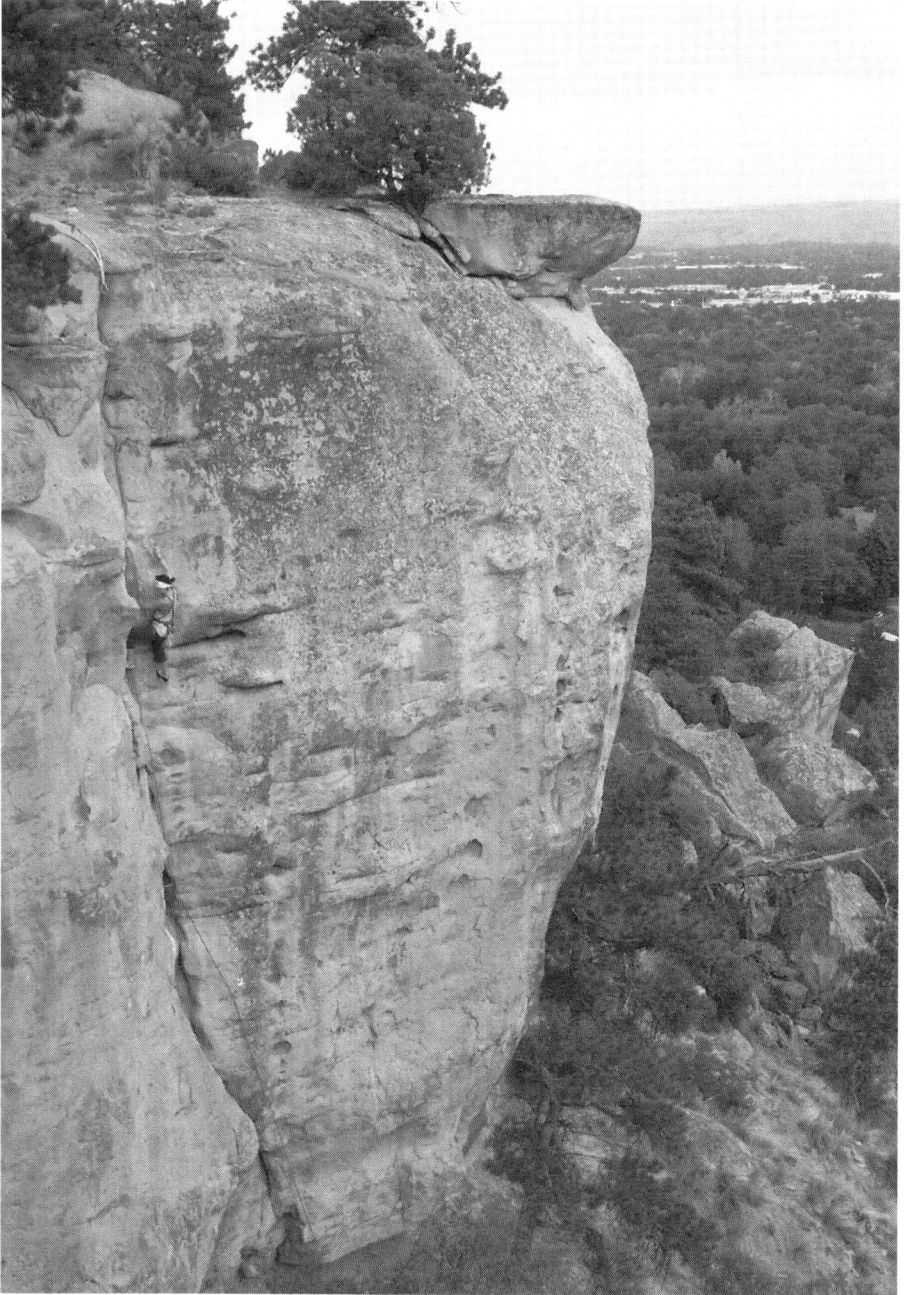

Mel Barbour on lead on The Tree Route.

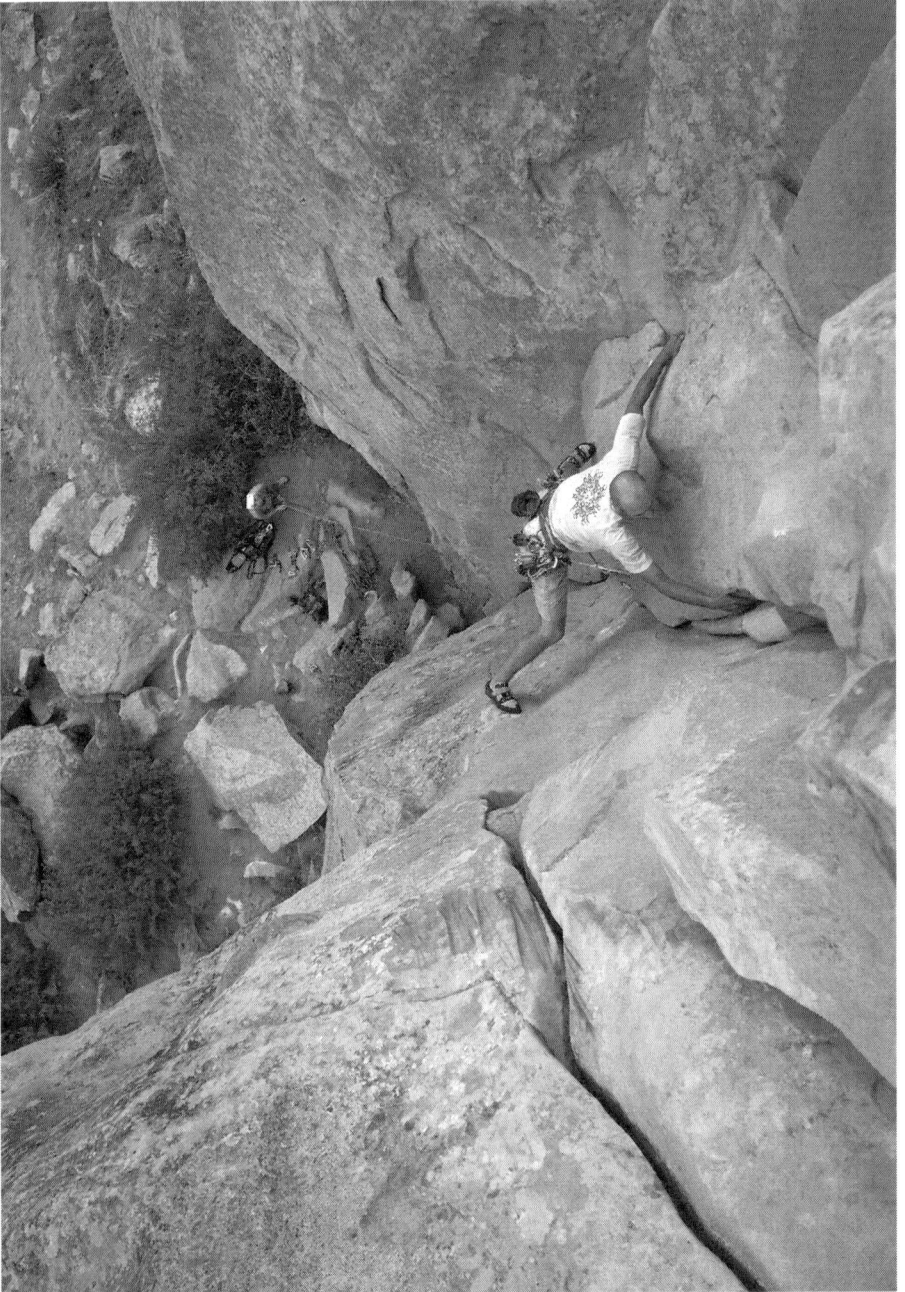

Daniel Burson climbing Barney Rubble

BARNEY RUBBLE AREA

1. Prime Rib 5.9***
The rare sporty moderate face climb on the rims. Bolts, bolts for anchors.

2. Barney Rubble Left 5.7***
Climb the corner crack and exit left at the mini-roof. Fun moderate climbing.
Trad climb, bolt (1) for anchors.

3. Barney Rubble 5.9****
Climb the corner crack up into steeper terrain and exit up left. A Billings Classic.
Trad Climb, bolts for anchors.

4. Roof Right 5.8***
A nice crack line terminates into a mini roof and thin crux finish. Trad Climb, bolt, bolts for anchors.

5. Mountaineers Route 5.6**
Just slightly more difficult than The Walkup. Climb a low angle crack into a steeper layback finish.
Trad Climb, bolts for anchors.

6. Blue in the Face 5.10a*
Start on Mountaineers Route and then climb the water streak on the face right.
Top rope, creativity required for the anchors.

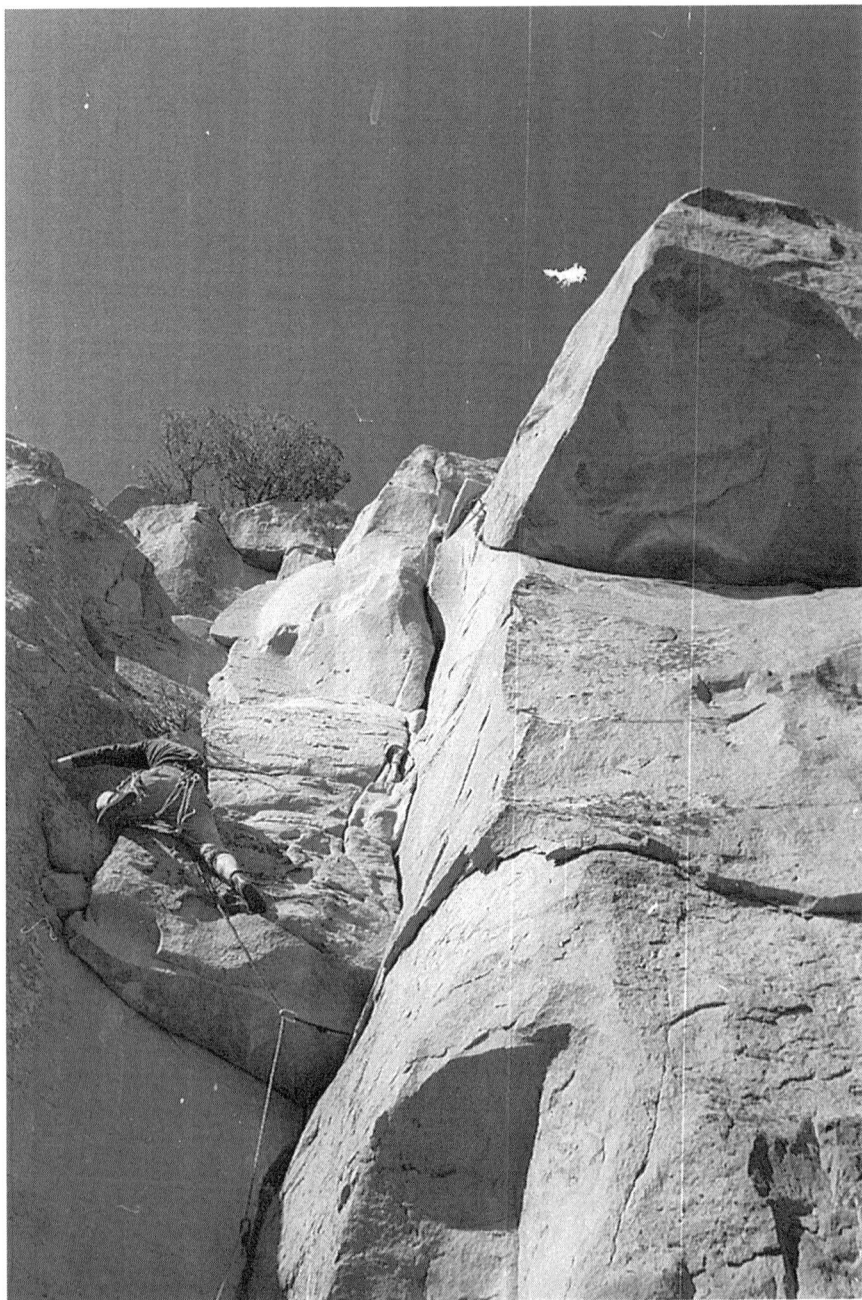

Chad Chadwick climbing Barney Rubble Left in 1967 (photo: Chadwick collection)

Chad skipping the pro on Roof Right in 1967 (photo: Chadwick collection)

SAPSUCKER AREA

1. I Don't Care 5.11a
Wandering route up a water streak.
Top Rope, make your own anchors.

2. Castles Made of Sand 5.11a
Start up Sapsucker and make a quick
exit left onto the face and thin holds.
Top Rope, make your own anchors.

3. Sapsucker 5.9***
A great crack climb that starts in a
flare and finishes on thin hands. Trad
climb, bolts for anchors.

4. The Ramp Crack 5.7
Climb up the crack that ramps up to
near vertical. Needs some gardening.
Trad climb, make your own anchors.

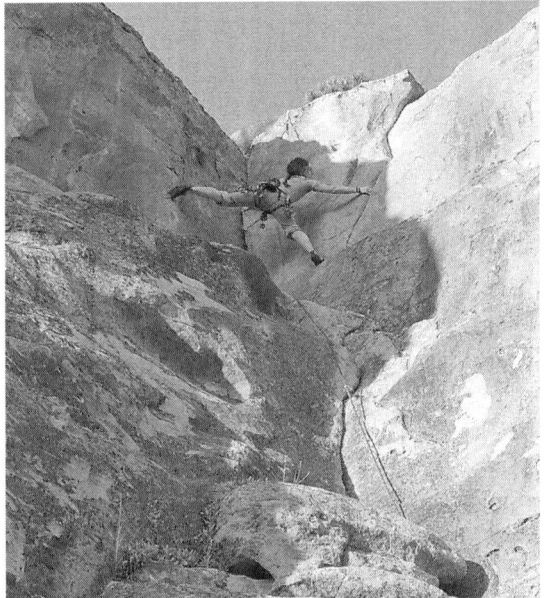

Anya Fiechtl leading up the Mountaineers Route

EXCUSE ABUSE AREA

1. Excuse Abuse 5.11b****
One of the best crack lines at Gregory. Thin fingers at the bottom into a great steep hand crack. The crux thin crack section can be circumnavigated on face holds to the right and drops the grade to 10d. Trad climb, bolts for anchors.

2. T & A 5.11a**
Climb the proud arete right of Excuse Abuse. The first bolt is up high. Bolts, the first is high and off route to the left. Sport climb, bolts for anchors.

3. Burning Down the Garage 5.9*
Start as for T&A, 20 feet up traverse right around the corner, and finish up the face. Good route that could use more traffic. Top rope, bolts for anchors, use the tree as a directional.

4. Last Best Route in Billings 5.12a*
See next page.

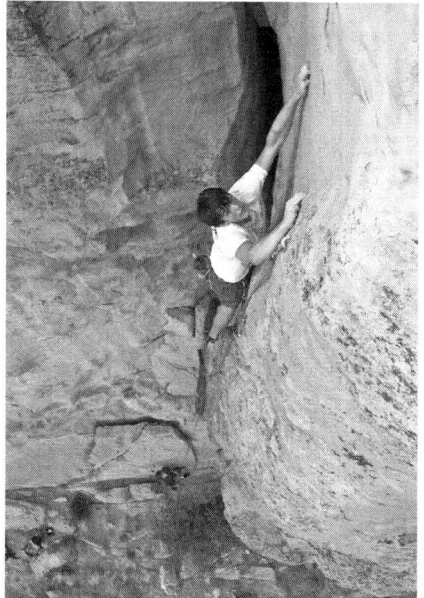

Charlie Barron on T & A

EVENING SHADE AREA

1. The Last Best Route in Billings 5.12a*
Start in a crack on the left side of the arete just east of T&A. Climb the crack, up through a thin face, then turn the corner to the right aiming for the obvious swiss cheese pockets, and top out. Top rope, bolts for anchors.

2. Next to Last Best Route in Billings 5.11c**
Start in a crack east and around the corner from The Last Best Route. Climb the crack into a steep face. Top rope, bolts for anchors.

3. Bumblie with a Drill 5.9+**
The easier of the two open book corners next to each other. Climb the crack and take the left corner. Trad climb, share the bolts with Get Up That Crack for the anchors.

4. Get Up that Crack 5.10b***
Start the same as for Bumblie with a Drill but take the right corner. Finish the same as for Bumblie, a direct finish is possible if you set the anchors up properly. Gear and bolts but commonly top roped. Bolts for anchors.

5. Eating Paisley 5.11a*
See next page.

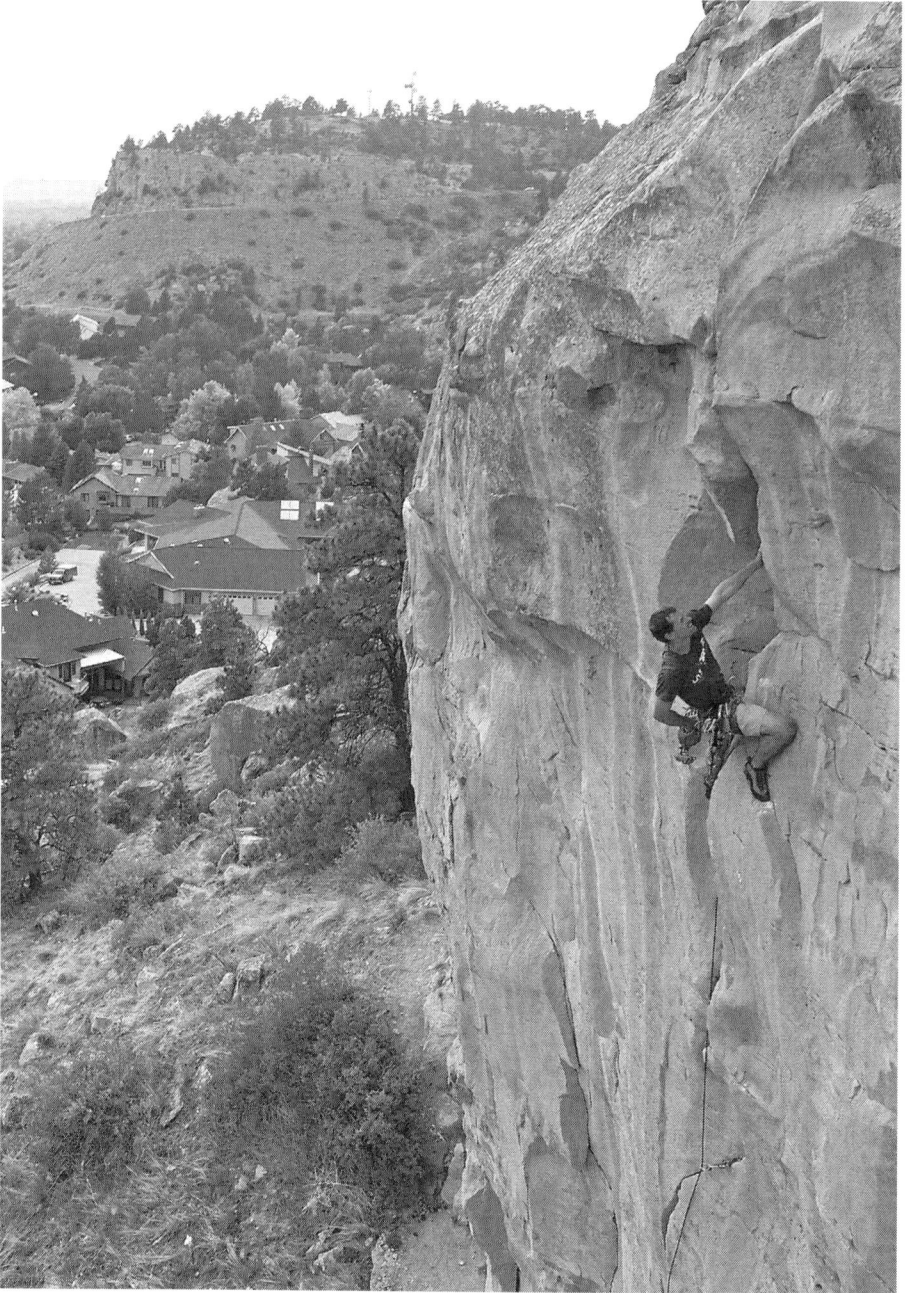

Rusty Willis has no excuse not to lead Excuse Abuse

EVENING SHADE AREA

1. Born to Hang 5.10a***
Climb the face without using the face to the right. Top rope, bolts for anchors.

2. Born to Climb 5.8**
Climb the corner and widening crack right of Born to Hang. Use the anchors from Born to Hang.

3. Slabarriffic 5.5*
An easy bolted route for access to the top. Sport climb, bolts for anchors.

4. Eating Paisley 5.11a*
Climb the water streak on the face right of Slabarrific. Top rope, make your own anchors.

EVENING SHADE AREA

A. Access Path
This path provides legal access to the routes at Gregory Hills without crossing any private property.

3. Slabarriffic 5.5*
An easy bolted route for access to the top. Sport climb, bolts for anchors.

4. Eating Paisley 5.11a*
Climb the water streak on the face right of Slabarrific. Top rope, make your own anchors.

5. Bumblie with a Drill 5.9+**
Trad climb, share the bolts with Get Up That Crack for the anchors. See page 100.

The rims are like a liquid. They take the shape of their container, and we're the containers.

Easy there Boss

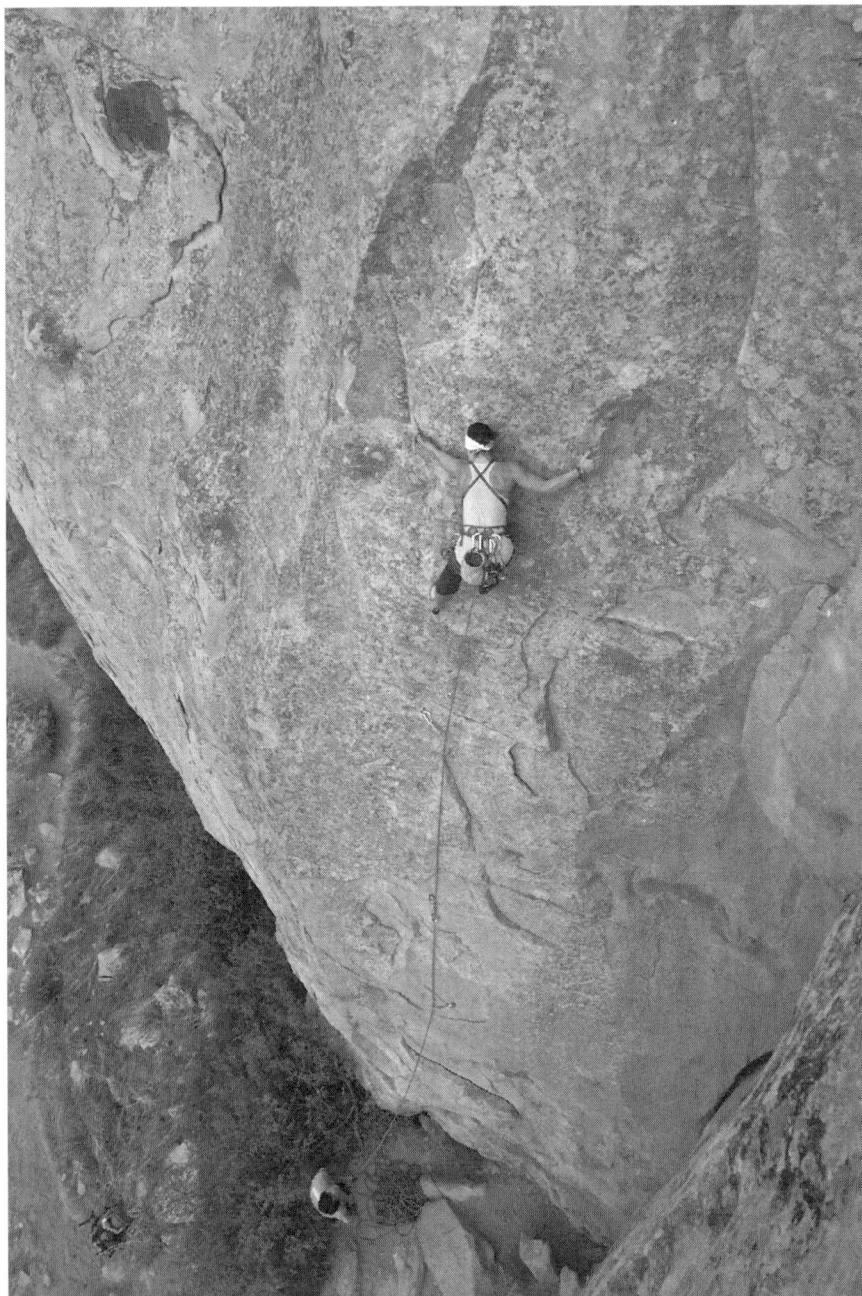

Mel Barbour climbing Prime Rib.

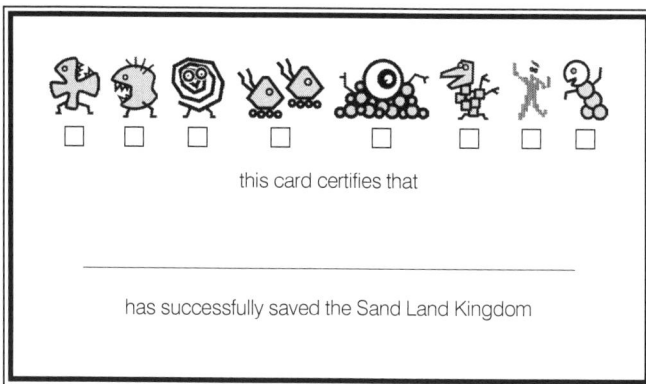

this card certifies that

_____

has successfully saved the Sand Land Kingdom

The Sand Monster
BONUS BOSS LEVEL

After defeating his Evil Henchmen you've earned the right to take on the Sand Monster himself.
Climb these routes to defeat the Sand Monster for good.

[ ] Be Bop Deluxe 5.12a
[ ] Tenacious 5.12a
[ ] Big Eagle Feather 5.11b
[ ] Mr. Chips 5.12c
[ ] Next to Last Best 5.11c

[ ] Just Do It V6
[ ] Rocky Top Orange Soda V5
[ ] Heath Bar Crunch V8
[ ] Lower Arvin Traverse V8
[ ] High Friction V7
[ ] Pregnant Mare V5

[ ] Fall of Man V6
[ ] Throw Your Hands Up V5
[ ] Ryan's Sloper Problem V8
[ ] Billings Radio 5.11d
[ ] Reubens Brother 5.11d